POVERTY AND ETHNICITY IN THE UK

Lucinda Platt

First published in Great Britain in 2007 by

The Policy Press
Fourth Floor, Beacon House
Queen's Road
Bristol BS8 1QU
UK

Tel no   +44 (0)117 331 4054
Fax no   +44 (0)117 331 4093
Email   tpp-info@bristol.ac.uk
www.policypress.org.uk

© University of Essex 2007

Published for the Joseph Rowntree Foundation by The Policy Press

ISBN 978 1 86134 989 7

British Library Cataloguing in Publication Data
A catalogue record for this book is available from the British Library.

Library of Congress Cataloging-in-Publication Data
A catalog record for this book has been requested.

Lucinda Platt is Senior Lecturer in Sociology in the Institute for Social and Economic
Research at the University of Essex.

The Joseph Rowntree Foundation has supported this project as part of its programme of
research and innovative development projects, which it hopes will be of value to policy
makers, practitioners and service users. The facts presented and views expressed in this
publication are, however, those of the author and not necessarily those of the Foundation.

The statements and opinions contained within this publication are solely those of the
author and not of the University of Bristol or The Policy Press. The University of Bristol
and The Policy Press disclaim responsibility for any injury to persons or property resulting
from any material published in this publication.

The Policy Press works to counter discrimination on grounds of gender, race, disability, age
and sexuality.

Cover design by Qube Design Associates, Bristol
Printed in Great Britain by Hobbs the Printers, Southampton

POVERTY AND ETHNICITY IN THE UK

Contents

List of figures and tables

Figures

Tables

Acknowledgements

I am grateful to the Joseph Rowntree Foundation (JRF) for funding this project. Helen Barnard and Chris Goulden from the JRF guided it and engaged energetically with the various issues that its execution raised. I am also grateful to all the members of the advisory group for giving their time to it and for their valuable comments and insights: Sarah Isal, Heidi Mirza, Chris Myant, Gina Netto, Ann Phoenix, Peter Ratcliffe, Krishna Sarda, Afsana Shukur and Nii Djan Tackey. Richard Berthoud also offered detailed and helpful feedback on the draft. Participants at the seminar for the preliminary dissemination of findings engaged in lively discussion and offered many additional thoughts and insights. Thanks to all of them. Some of this work was carried out while I was a visiting researcher at DIW Berlin and subsequently at the Centre for Analysis of Social Exclusion (CASE) at the London School of Economics and Political Science. I would like to thank both of these institutions for their hospitality. The book was both begun and ended at the University of Essex. I am grateful to the Sociology Department at the University of Essex for allowing the time to carry out this review and for the facilities and research support offered by the University of Essex. Judi Egerton, an information specialist, was the other member of the project team and continued to send me valuable references, as well as giving advice on searching and on Endnote, throughout the life of the project. I could not have done it without her.

Summary

Background and approach

This book represents a wide-ranging review of the literature relating to poverty and ethnicity commissioned by the Joseph Rowntree Foundation, which has identified stark differences in rates of poverty according to ethnic group. The review brings together all the available evidence on different aspects of poverty and examines what has (and has not) been studied in relation to its causes.

The review explored evidence on poverty and ethnicity, employing a flexible approach to ethnicity, and also touching on related issues such as migrant background and religious affiliation. Thousands of studies were screened for potential inclusion and evidence and 350 were selected for review in the final book. Most of the studies identified used the Census categories (sometimes with modifications to take account of religious affiliation or whether born in Britain), and there was little distinct analysis of White groups.

The framework for the review prioritised an income measure of poverty as being most transparent and as allowing for consideration of different components of income. Deprivation was conceived as stemming from lack of income, at least in the long term. However, evidence on material deprivation measures, as distinct from income, was also included and reviewed to the extent that it was available.

Ethnic differences in rates of poverty

The review found that all identified minority ethnic groups had higher rates of poverty than the average for the population. Rates of poverty were highest for Bangladeshis, Pakistanis and Black Africans, reaching nearly two thirds for Bangladeshis. Rates of poverty were also higher for those living in Indian, Chinese and other minority ethnic group households.

These differences were found, and in roughly the same order, when sub-populations such as pensioners or children were considered. For example, Indian and Caribbean pensioners were poorer than White pensioners and Pakistani pensioners were poorer than Indian pensioners. Child poverty rates were greater than adult poverty rates across groups, so that children from minority ethnic groups were poorer both than White children and than adults from their own ethnic groups. Around 70% of Bangladeshi children were found to be poor.

Differences in poverty by ethnic group were also found when using different measures of poverty and deprivation, such as lack of material goods and duration of poverty, as well as income insecurity. Deprivation is a wide-ranging term, and what it summarises varies from study to study. It can cover a lack of material possessions, such as warm clothing; housing stress, such as leaky roofs; opportunities for social activity, such as having friends round; anxiety about making ends meet; or some combination. It thus means slightly different things depending on the context. Nevertheless, Bangladeshis were identified as having the greatest poverty for most measures. Poverty for this group also appeared to be severer and more long-lasting than that experienced by other groups.

Pakistanis were found to be nearly as poor as Bangladeshis on many counts, but there appeared to be differences in degree. Pakistanis also appeared to have rather different patterns of material deprivation. For example, one study of childhood deprivation found that Bangladeshi children were highly likely to be deprived, but Pakistani children were not especially likely to be among the most deprived. Instead, Black African children were identified as being the second most deprived group.

Levels of social contact and money worries showed rather different patterns across the ethnic groups. Bangladeshis and Pakistanis did not appear to be deprived in relation to informal social contact; but Black Caribbeans and Black Africans, especially women from these groups, did. And Caribbeans experienced the greatest levels of anxiety about finances. In addition, even though those from White groups were least likely to be in poverty, among those White British claiming means-tested benefits, low-income persistence was found to be greatest.

Thus, although there is broad consistency in the 'poverty ranking' of ethnic groups, its expression in particular areas reveals some differences.

In addition to extensive variation in experience between groups, there is also substantial variation within groups that is not adequately captured by existing categories. Recognition of within-group diversity challenges forms of explanation based around ethnicity or religious affiliation. The intersection between these two can also complicate our understanding of disadvantage. Nevertheless, recognition of diversity should not detract from the high risks of poverty associated with particular ethnic identities or categories.

Differences in components of income: savings, benefits and earnings

There was evidence of ethnic differences across sources of income: from employment, from savings and assets, and from benefit income. Many minority ethnic groups had no savings, although the Indian group was an exception. The contribution of benefits to household income has not been analysed by ethnic group, but minority ethnic groups had lower rates of receipt of contributory benefits. Some groups were, instead, high users of means-tested benefits, which imply low incomes in the first place. There were, nevertheless, questions about the extent to which some minority ethnic groups actually claimed or received their entitlement to benefits (take-up).

It was clear that income from employment was a central issue in determining poverty. It impacted on those of all ages, including those of pension age: lifetime employment record and earnings affected the amount of pension income older people received; and there were clear differences in the extent to which different ethnic groups had private pension provision. In addition, pensioners do not necessarily live alone – and indeed, multi-generation households are much more common among Pakistani, Bangladeshi and Indian households. Thus, older people could benefit from, or suffer from, the extent to which those of working age in the same household were in (well-paid) employment.

There were large differences in employment rates across ethnic groups. Unemployment rates were higher for all identified minority ethnic groups compared to the majority and economic inactivity rates also varied widely. Rates of pay also differed substantially, with Bangladeshi men facing particularly low rates of pay. This meant that both in-work and out-of-work Bangladeshi households faced high poverty risks.

Understanding differences in poverty

Analysis of employment disadvantage found that it could partly be explained by characteristics such as education, but that an ethnic penalty tended to remain. The term 'ethnic penalty' is used to summarise the disadvantage associated with a particular ethnic category that remains once relevant characteristics have been controlled for. It therefore encompasses additional, unmeasured, factors including discrimination. This was the case both for chances of being in a job and for rates of pay, although the ethnic penalty for being in employment was more important. Ethnic penalties varied across groups. Despite high levels of qualifications Black Africans were not achieving the employment outcomes that would be expected to accompany such qualifications. Indians also faced a penalty relative to their employable characteristics. Taking account of characteristics reduced the employment gap for Pakistanis and Bangladeshis, but a substantial ethnic penalty was still found. This was particularly the case for Pakistanis. Although they did not appear quite as poor as the Bangladeshis, the ethnic penalties they faced often appeared more intractable.

The other side of the equation to income is needs. That is, the demands on available income. Household sizes were substantially higher than average for Bangladeshi, Pakistani and Indian households, meaning there were greater demands on available income. Lone-parent families were much more prevalent among Black African and Black Caribbean households. Lone-parent households are known to have higher risks of poverty due to the pressures of combining work and childcare for lone parents. While mothers in lone-parent Black African and Black Caribbean households are more likely to be in employment than those in other households, this does not necessarily allow them to avoid poverty; and it may impact on other aspects of welfare such as social contacts. Rates of sickness and disability were much higher among Bangladeshi households. Sick and disabled people have low employment rates; and they can also reduce the employment options for their carers. Moreover, the extra costs associated with disability were not typically taken into account in estimates of poverty, which may suggest even higher (or more severe) poverty for these households than already observed. Costs of living also showed some variation by ethnic group.

Policy implications

The implications for policy are twofold. First, it is important to increase income from employment for poor families, which will also have knock-on effects in later life. Second, there are issues around effective income maintenance for poor households. Given the agenda to eliminate child poverty, this can be seen as particularly important for households with children.

In order to address the high poverty risks experienced by certain ethnic groups, employment policies need to address the following areas: employer discrimination; making work pay; retention in employment; and using 'welfare to work' to focus on helping people to move into a stable job with progression prospects rather than 'any job'.

However, focusing solely on employment will not address all the causes of poverty and its differences by ethnicity. Other relevant policy agendas are those relating to benefits and to skills. Take-up of benefit by those eligible needs to be made a greater priority. Also, further consideration needs to be given to the extent to which the contributory system can systematically disadvantage certain population groups. The adequacy of benefits, particularly for those engaged in caring or with multiple caring roles, also needs to be given further attention.

Moreover, there needs to be sensitivity towards the costs (as well as the benefits) in terms of potential isolation or family welfare, as well as the benefits of economic activity, particularly where the opportunities and rewards are limited.

In addition, while there are many policy agendas that are relevant to tackling poverty among minority ethnic groups, for example around employment and job search, childcare, area initiatives and discrimination, it is important that policy is followed through at the level of procedures and practices on the ground, and that it can be shown to be meeting the needs of the target populations.

Informing policy

In a number of areas knowledge remains partial, and further research is necessary if policy is to be able to respond appropriately and effectively to the major challenge of ethnic differences in poverty. The lack of a sufficiently detailed evidence base is most striking in relation to the extent and depth of investigation into ethnic differences in poverty and deprivation itself; and therefore it is harder to arrive at firm conclusions about appropriate interventions. Many of the studies drawn on are limited, or relatively old, while up-to-date figures from Households Below Average Income (HBAI) (DWP, 2005a) only provide the broad outlines of the issue. Much of the evidence drawn on in the book thus related to employment, pay or other related areas such as experience of benefits. The relative role of income maintenance policies and the importance of work and pay cannot be properly understood, nor initiatives addressed unless we understand the extent to which they contribute to differences in poverty rates.

Other issues that demand further investigation to improve our understanding and refine policy responses are:

- composition of income in households of different ethnic groups and in different types of household (for example, those with children, those with sick and disabled members, pensioner households);
- the extent and processes of employer discrimination;
- the extent of non–take–up of benefits as it varies by type of benefit and ethnic group;
- the ways in which understandings of poverty (and of related issues such as class) have or may have different meanings for those with different ethnic identities and the implications of such differences;
- more detailed investigation of inter–household income transfers or obligations and their impacts;
- a developed understanding of the role of social networks and ethnic capital (understood as the overall levels of human capital within a group) in promoting (or inhibiting) upward mobility and life chances for minority ethnic groups.

ONE

Introduction

This book is the result of a review of literature on ethnicity and poverty commissioned by the Joseph Rowntree Foundation and which started in April, 2005. The content of the book covers a summary of findings from research explicitly covering poverty and ethnicity and a longer discussion on the sources of these poverty rates, drawing on research reported since 1991, with a particular focus on the most recent papers. In this introduction I rehearse the aims and rationale of the study, cover the methodology and consider issues surrounding the study's scope and coverage.

Aims and rationale

The purpose of this book is to outline the current state of knowledge in relation to poverty and ethnicity. That is, to describe, in so far as there is information, differences in poverty rates and experiences according to ethnic group, being sensitive to differences within groups, and the definitions of groups. These latter issues are discussed at more length in Chapter Two, which set out to look at what we know about how poverty varies across groups and what we know about how it is experienced within groups.

Both of these – heterogeneity between groups and heterogeneity within groups – are important considerations when examining poverty. Heterogeneity between groups tells us about relative disadvantage and about inequalities within society. Looking at poverty rates and differences between groups can be important in helping to understand what are the aspects of ethnicity – or the factors or characteristics associated with belonging to a particular ethnic group – that lead to greater or lesser poverty. That is, it can help us to unpick the meaning and 'role' of ethnicity in affecting outcomes. In that sense, such heterogeneity is also an important element in refining any attempt to explain or account for ethnic differences in poverty. Examining heterogeneity within groups can be valuable in helping us to understand how poverty is experienced differently by those with different clusters of characteristics; what it means to particular groups and whether this is the same as it means to other groups, what its impacts are and what other aspects of lived experience have the potential to ameliorate or intensify it. For example, does the intensity of the experience of poverty vary according to whether your reference group is more or less poor? (And who is that reference group anyway? Neighbours? Those in the same 'class position' as yourself? Those of the same ethnic group or nationality as yourself?) Both poverty and ethnicity are still somewhat black boxes in relation to exactly how they impact on certain outcomes and life chances. Exploring poverty within groups – both how it varies and how it is experienced – could help us to understand more about both of these. In the event, the review identified little research that looks within groups at the experience of poverty. The fields of both poverty and ethnicity research are rich and varied in their own right – but the gains to be made from bringing them together in this way have not been extensively explored. This remains an issue for the research agenda if we are to complement our understanding of the brute inequalities revealed by comparison between groups with some understanding of what they mean more specifically for the individuals concerned.

The focus of this book is, therefore, of necessity more on comparisons of poverty across ethnic groups and the variation in other characteristics across groups that can help to account for differences in poverty. By bringing together this knowledge, the aim is that messages for policy in relation to mitigating poverty or confronting its causes will become apparent. Moreover, identifying the gaps in that knowledge will indicate where understanding is insufficiently clear to inform policy, and the need for further investigation. Comparisons across groups tend to require a point of reference to which comparison can be made. This will typically be the average or the experience of the White majority. Although there are risks in such an approach of 'normalising' the experience of the majority (discussed further in Chapter Two), it is hard to avoid and is standard among much of the literature summarised. In the case of poverty comparisons, it may, anyway, be more justifiable in that on almost every measure that has been employed and where ethnic differences have been considered the majority experiences lower poverty rates than any other group. Thus, political imperatives associated with poverty demand a greater attention to ameliorating the poverty of the minority ethnic groups, even if there are acknowledged risks of pathologising them or of 'blaming the victim' that go with that.

Since the Cantle Report into the disturbances in the North of England (Community Cohesion Review Team, 2001), there has been a strong policy stress on social cohesion as the central challenge facing not only new immigrant communities but also longstanding minority ethnic groups (Home Office, 2004a, 2005a). The concept of 'community cohesion is based on ideological assumptions (Robinson, 2005); and a feature of this current discourse is that it has a strong assimilationist tendency, replacing a former stress on diversity and multiculturalism as the centre of race relations policy (Alam and Husband, 2006). Further, it has emphasised the centrality of social relations at the expense of a focus on equality and economic integration (Zetter et al, 2006).

On the other hand re-recognition of economic disadvantage being central to minority ethnic groups' experience has, both in the past and again more recently, tended to reinforce perceptions of minorities as alien or outsiders. Unemployment and economic disadvantage have reappeared in the Home Office's community cohesion strategy as well as in the more longstanding focus within the Department for Work and Pensions on minimising the 'ethnic employment gap', but with the particular slant that not paying attention to economic inequality is now regarded as risking putting strains on 'social cohesion' (Open Society Institute EU Monitoring and Advocacy Program, 2004). Thus, economic integration becomes identified with an assimiliationist approach to inclusion.

This book is concerned with economic inequalities and the intense deprivation suffered by certain ethnic groups relative to others in the UK today. It is based on the premise that inequalities and highly different risks of poverty are a concern for society in and of themselves. It is not concerned to claim that economic integration is a means either to social harmony or to eliminate difference. Indeed, the reduction of poverty may aid expression of difference: insofar as poverty limits opportunity, it also limits opportunity of expression and that includes the ability to realise difference and felt identity. Instead, the concern here is with social justice. The deleterious consequences of poverty for life chances and its impact on multiple aspects of life are well documented (Ermisch et al, 2001; Flaherty et al, 2004; Pantazis et al, 2006). The recognition of poverty brings with it an expectation of action (Alcock, 2006), that it is a state of affairs to be remedied. When this is accompanied by stark differences in the chances of experiencing or living in poverty, according to social divisions (Anthias, 2001; Payne, 2006), in this case that of ethnicity, then the imperative of poverty is linked to that of injustice and is consequently heightened. It is the existence, maintenance and even extension of polarisation and of inequality within society that make ethnic group disadvantage possible – not vice versa. Cultural or ethnic difference is, for the purposes of this review, of particular interest or concern only in so far as it is associated with differential life chances. From this perspective, then, the justification for examining ethnic differences in poverty is that there *are* large differences.

The review also set out to attempt to understand the causes of that poverty and of the differences in poverty. As the book shows, there is no one cause that can predominantly explain differences in poverty rates, nor are the combinations of causes and their relative weights the same for different groups. Thus, for example, relatively low skills leading to more limited employment opportunities is an issue for some groups, but not others.

The rationale of the book, then, is to identify the extent to which there are differences in risks or experience of poverty by ethnic group; to attempt to understand where such differences stem from in order to inform policies that can tackle them; and to identify where our knowledge is not adequate to the task of informing poverty either because we do not know enough about the nature and extent of poverty in certain areas or because we do not understand well enough what is driving it or how factors link together.

The book is structured as follows. The rest of this chapter covers the methodology of the review, its coverage in principle and practice, and its structure and organising framework. Part One examines conceptual and definitional issues. Chapter Two looks at those issues relating to definitions of ethnicity and the scope and treatment of ethnic groups for the purpose of this book (picking up on some of the issues of coverage discussed in this chapter); while Chapter Three examines definitional and conceptual issues relating to poverty.

Part Two consists of one chapter (Chapter Four) (with multiple subdivisions), which considers the raw 'facts' of poverty and its differentiation by ethnic group. It considers variation according to different measures of poverty – to the extent that evidence is available – and also in the component aspects of income as outlined in the structural framework in this introduction. In the chapter there is no attempt to control for differences in the situation of groups, other than by giving broad breakdowns for subpopulations such as children. Instead, the focus is on absolute differences regardless of where they stem from.

Part Three, by contrast, focuses on potential explanations and thus draws on the literature that attempts to 'compare like with like' (although on the problems of such an approach see Platt, 2006d), or to investigate the role played in differences in outcomes by particular characteristics. Chapter Five focuses on analysis of employment and earnings and the linked role of educational qualifications while Chapter Six concentrates on demographic issues and aspects of household structure. Chapter Seven examines the role of social security.

Part Four concludes the book by considering, briefly, the policy implications of existing research (Chapter Eight) and the gaps in knowledge and understanding that can be used to frame a future research agenda (Chapter Nine).

Methodology

This review aimed to comprehensively garner information on and relating to poverty and ethnicity in the UK. While it explicitly did not set out to be a 'systematic review' of the form that is currently widely in vogue (see discussion paper on systematic reviewing on the project website)[1], it did aim to use a far-reaching search strategy, which was laid out in a draft protocol. This strategy included online databases, web searches, reference checking, contacts with researchers in the field and so on. (See relevant papers on the project website for more details.) Specialist advice was sought on the strategy itself and was incorporated into the approach for implementing it. The review also drew on systematic approaches by defining the period of reference (only literature from 1991 onwards was incorporated), by the area of reference (by including only literature covering the UK) and by using some quality evaluation of the research that was completed for each article or paper read. Much of the quality evaluation in fact revolved around identifying redundancy (including eliminating duplicate versions of basically the same paper, for example, for working papers and published versions): the most recent version was the one selected in such cases.

While there is little direct analysis of poverty and ethnicity, as this book illustrates, there is a wealth of literature on areas that are potentially related: different aspects of employment and quality of life, education, neighbourhood and so on. The searches threw up literally thousands of references, which were screened initially to exclude obviously irrelevant ones on the basis of date, subject or country of focus. Preliminary broad reading was then used to build up a sense of the field, from which a structure for the book and the issues it needed to cover was developed. This structure was then itself used to inform the selection and incorporation of references, and further, more targeted, searching. Circularity of reference points was used to indicate a level of saturation, which showed that the targeted field had been covered. Thus, the approach used could be said to approximate to a form of theoretical searching. Material that fell outside the geographical coverage of the project was incorporated where it provided a valuable theoretical or explanatory framework that contributed to the overall account. Such material was included sparingly, however.

The review also used the author's knowledge of the poverty literature more generally to identify material that contained some ethnic group analysis, but where that analysis was sufficiently minor that it would not have been picked up by systematic searches. The advisory group was also drawn on to provide a check on the coverage and comprehensiveness of the book. The result is a detailed discussion of existing information on poverty and ethnicity, with wide coverage of factors that need to be considered in understanding that information, as far as research has developed. These can be used in understanding policy implications and the limitations of existing research both in enabling understanding of ethnic differences in poverty and in informing the developing policy agenda. In coverage it goes beyond the only recent work specifically on this topic (Platt, 2002). It is also very up to date with references reaching to just before the point at which the writing was completed (end 2006). This incorporation of very recent references goes against not only the principles of systematic review, but also the original plan for this review, where searching was intended to end in December 2005. Active searches did cease around that point, but 2006 was a very rich year for publications relating to relevant aspects of ethnic group experience and diversity and it was felt that it would have been perverse, and substantially reduced the review's utility, credibility and impact, to have ignored such publications.

As it is, the review is well placed to provide the basis for analysis of policy and to inform current and future research agendas. The final chapter sets out the immediate implications of its findings.

Nevertheless, despite its breadth, comprehensiveness and authority, this review must be read as necessarily affected by the interests, biases and ontological positioning of the author. It was also influenced by pragmatic considerations relating to the best use of necessarily limited resources. Moreover, there are some areas that readers might consider relevant to issues of poverty that have not been addressed in this book, for example the position of looked-after children and the experience of custody and imprisonment.

Coverage: temporal, geographical and ethnic

The extent of poverty and disadvantage among the minority ethnic groups of the UK has long been a source of interest. Alongside such seminal, local investigations as Rex's work in Birmingham (Rex and Moore, 1967), national studies which highlighted some of the main features of Britain's minority ethnic group populations and the disadvantage they experienced were carried out approximately every decade from the 1960s, first by Political and Economic Planning and then by the Policy Studies Institute (Daniel, 1968; Smith, 1977; Brown, 1984; Modood et al, 1997). In addition, some major general sources for analysing and understanding life chances of individuals with different characteristics contained information on ethnic group for a substantial period, for example the Labour Force Survey has reported versions of ethnic group questions since 1979. Nevertheless, even by 1992 and the publication of what might be considered the first overview of poverty and ethnicity (Amin and Oppenheim, 1992), sources were limited and the information on poverty was often by association rather than direct.

The year 1991 can be seen as marking a watershed in the availability of sources for analysis of certain ethnic groups with the incorporation into the Census of an ethnic group question,[2] accompanied by the increasing use of the question across other sources. The year 1991, therefore, provides the start date for the review of the literature contained in this book. Analyses that are solely based on data deriving from before 1991 are excluded even if they were not published until after 1991. Clearly, the tabulations and analyses based on the Census itself did not appear until somewhat after 1991, but the date is still considered a convenient cut-point because of the change in thinking that also accompanies the introduction of an ethnic group question (Bonnett and Carrington, 2000), and which will thus have an impact from around that time.

There have also been further important developments in data and thinking around ethnicity and classification since 1991. These have included another Census with another, different, ethnic group question, and the reporting of results from that. Thus, in this book, preference has tended to be given to more recent rather than earlier material, and this will be reflected in the weighting of the discussion.

The landmark nature of the 1991 Census question and the range and depth of information that it could provide on diversity within as well as between classified minority ethnic groups were celebrated in the production of a four-volume series on the characteristics and experiences of Britain's minority ethnic groups (Coleman and Salt, 1996a; Peach, 1996a; Ratcliffe, 1996a; Karn, 1997). This wealth of data and analysis provides an invaluable context for understanding the position of the nine Census categories of minority ethnic groups, with some limited analysis of the UK's White minorities (Chance, 1996; Compton, 1996).[3]

Although they have information on health, housing, employment, education and household structure, decennial Censuses have so far contained no information on income, and thus no direct information on individual or household poverty. The crucial development for the purpose of measuring (income) poverty by ethnic group was the introduction of the Family Resources Survey in 1993, with much larger sample sizes than the Family Expenditure Survey, very detailed income questions and an ethnic group question. Low-income statistics in the form of HBAI measures were subsequently produced from this source, giving annual updates on income poverty rates by ethnic group as well as by a range of other characteristics.

More recently, however, and particularly with the effects of devolution and the creation of new administrations in Wales and Scotland, there has been increasing interest in the different countries of the UK. This has drawn attention to differences in experiences between as well as within these countries, and to the distinctiveness of elements of the often homogenised, 'White' population. It has also revealed the lack of much truly UK-wide research on ethnic differences in outcomes. For example, the Census volumes mentioned above covered the British Census. Given the difference in questions between Britain and Northern Ireland, they exclude Northern Ireland with the exception of the discussion in Compton (1996). And despite its title, Modood et al's (1997) study of *Ethnic Minorities in Britain* only covers England and Wales. Moreover, the 2001 Census in Scotland had a different ethnic group question from that used in England and Wales, and thus analysis from that Census has been carried out separately for Scotland (Scottish Executive, 2004). Similarly, Census results for Northern Ireland are available separately and cover slightly different groups (most notably including Irish Travellers as a distinct category) from those for the other countries (see http://www.nicensus2001.gov.uk/).

Gaps in national analysis alongside the need, enhanced by devolution, to produce country-based analyses of various population characteristics including ethnicity for the different countries (Brown, U., 2000) has extensively increased the knowledge base both about poverty within these countries and about diversity within their populations. For example, Netto et al (2001) conducted a 'race' audit of both key issues, and sources and gaps in research. (See also Bowes and Sim, 1997, and the summary of projects in the Scottish Executive's Research Bulletin and its analysis of ethnicity in the 2001 Census – Scottish Executive, 2001, 2004.) In relation to Wales, a 'Focus' on Wales highlights the characteristics of Wales, including 'living standards' and ethnic group composition (ONS, 2004), and a 'Statistical Focus' provides a detailed breakdown of ethnicity in Wales (National Statistics, 2004a); even though most of the standard key statistics from the 2001 Census cover both England and Wales together.

This book therefore aims to be clear about what is the geographical coverage of any given study (to the extent that it is made clear in the source), and to be sensitive to differences across countries within the UK as far as is possible. The difficulty of achieving effective comparative analysis across the countries of the UK can be illustrated, however, by the fact that in their recent analysis of employment penalties, Berthoud and Blekesaune (2006) had to pool 10 years of the General Household Survey to compare penalties for most of the vulnerable groups across England, Wales and Scotland, and even here there were insufficient cases to conduct a comparative analysis of ethnic employment penalties. Despite its aim for UK coverage, research does not yet exist that allows even coverage across the UK and meaningful comparison across its countries.

Similarly, the aim to provide in this review coverage of issues of poverty in relation to White ethnicity was limited by the availability of research that took this as a point of investigation. On the other hand, the mainstream poverty literature is, by default (as a result of numerical dominance), predominantly an investigation of poverty experience within the White majority. Thus, this mainstream literature will provide the basis for understanding the diversity of experience, the polarisation between populations, the geographical variation and the diversity in poverty experience among the UK's White populations. It will also indicate relevant policy issues. It is clearly not the aim of this review to cover the general poverty literature (nor could it hope to). But, given the extensiveness of this literature and thus issues of poverty within the population as a whole and the majority in particular, it is only appropriate that this review should not focus extensively on White ethnicity, except where White minority groups are specifically distinguished.

A further impetus to examining a wider range of ethnic groups than those in the 1991 Census categories has come from changing patterns of and reasons for migration. Substantial migration from within Europe in recent years has invited further scrutiny of the 'White' population and a concern with the particular experience of new migrants, separating out issues of country of birth and period of migration from questions of ethnicity. One of these groups of new migrants are Roma from Central Europe. Roma have traditionally been subject to marginalisation in the nations they have lived in and between, and they have not escaped from vociferous anti-immigration attention in Britain, either. But the UK's own longstanding population of Roma or Gypsies and of Irish Travellers has been subject to pressure in terms of their ability to carry on their traditional life, while having been largely neglected in general discussions of poverty and disadvantage (Cemlyn and Clark, 2005). The government's poverty and opportunity agenda has acknowledged the particular situation and marginalisation of Traveller groups, as part of examining the European dimension of its strategy (DWP, 2005b, p 128). This review has set out to cover, as far as the research exists, both new migrants and Gypsies or Travellers. However, there remains very little available research that is directly related to the subject of this review, that is, their experience of poverty specifically.

In addition, the nature of new migration with the increasing prevalence of refugees, resulting from both widespread disruption in many parts of the world and changes in immigration law that restricted other forms of immigrant, has drawn attention to minority groups identified by their status – as asylum seekers – rather than by virtue of their ethnic group. I discuss these points further in the next chapter. Here I refer to them to indicate the extent to which what we might consider ethnicity overlaps with different categorisations and ways of organising people. Common to issues of ethnicity and immigration status are issues of power in relation to settled and immigrant status, issues of differentiation and issues of discrimination. Legal status and external construction are particularly significant for asylum seekers in the current hostile context; but, as I discuss further in the next chapter, processes of recognition are crucial to the construction of groups more widely. Although it does not make sense to consider asylum seekers as an ethnic group, and refugees are not explicitly covered in this book, the issue of their poverty draws attention to particular processes of racialisation and marginalisation that are implicit in social and political structures.

Finally, on the topic of coverage, it is important to note the emphasis that should be given in a book of this nature to intersectionality (Brah and Shaw, 1992), that is, to the interconnection of different potential sources of identity and disadvantage (see also the discussion in Alam and Husband, 2006), for example, the way that ethnicity and class interact to create deeper disadvantage, or the ways in which gender can mediate ethnic disadvantage. It is therefore important to examine issues of difference – and different sources of disadvantage – within and across ethnic groups. Most obviously, the distinctive patterning of poverty by sex across the population as a whole should be borne in mind. Gendered differences in the experience of poverty within and between groups are an important consideration for this study and some of these issues are picked up specifically in Chapter Six. But aspects of generation and class also cut across ethnic differences and reveal divergences within ethnicities that may be as great or greater than those between them. Even if ethnic group is used as the main form of grouping individuals and exploring differences in this book, it is important to state at the outset that it may not be the most important – or consistently the most important – means by which individuals classify themselves (Campbell and McLean, 2003).

Structure and framework

The framework of the book is illustrated in Figure 1.1. It illustrates in the circle the issue at the heart of the review: poverty, and who is poor. However, although low income is not necessarily identified with poverty, the figure also makes clear that income is regarded as a critical determinant of poverty. I discuss this issue further in Chapter Three where I briefly cover the different concepts and measures of poverty and the reason for this (not unproblematic) focus on household income. As a result, Chapter Four, the central chapter of the book, first considers evidence on household income poverty, highlighted in the central square box, and its distribution by ethnicity. It then goes on to consider, individually, the different

Figure 1.1: The causes of poverty

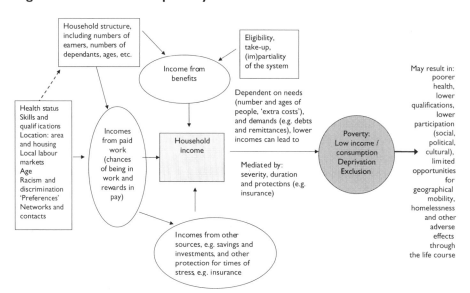

sources of household income as identified in the ovals (earnings, assets and benefit income), and how these vary with ethnicity.

However, Chapter Four also considers what direct evidence we have on deprivation and other ways of measuring poverty, in relation to ethnicity. It then reviews the evidence base on the factors that are seen to mediate the relationship between income and poverty, that is, at what point a given level of (household) income translates into poverty. These mediating factors are judged to be the demands on the income: at the simplest, how many people are expected to live off it. This is usually taken into account when measuring household income in the first place – what is cited and compared is adjusted household income – although, of course, the benefits of high income or costs of low household income may not be equally distributed across the household. Some members may lose out relative to others and others (such as children) may be 'protected' (Middleton and Ashworth, 1995). This issue is considered further both in Chapter Three on defining poverty and in Chapter Four. However, there may also be different demands on the income that effectively reduce it, or its value: extra costs, such as the extra costs stemming from disability, are one example, but there may also be extra costs associated with the situation of particular ethnic groups.

At the same time, the impact of low income will vary with the severity – the amount by which it is below any given poverty 'threshold' and by its duration: the longer low income lasts the more likely it is to affect living standards (Jenkins and Rigg, 2001). Therefore, Chapter Four also reviews the state of knowledge about duration and intensity of poverty and how that varies with ethnicity. Finally, it considers whether there is any evidence that what is understood as poverty itself varies with ethnicity. If, as is conventionally argued, poverty is a relational concept, then the point of reference may mean different understandings of poverty for different individuals. Different priorities may also impact on understandings of poverty. What implications do differences in belief have for our understanding of ethnic differences in poverty? Although there is little research in this area, it is an important consideration to bear in mind. After considering this question, the book moves on, in subsequent chapters, to look at what are the causes of the poverty rates illustrated.

Obviously, and as Figure 1.1 attempts to make clear, causes of poverty or the characteristics associated with lower incomes are various, complex and often interlinked. In addition, factors impacting on one area may have different consequences on another. To take the example of the role of family structure, a partner of a lone parent moving in with her/him may increase the earnings in a household but in the process may reduce the parent's benefit entitlement. The control over household or family income may also shift, as this example makes clear. Intra-household distribution of resources – although often noted – are still insufficiently well understood for drawing conclusions about the different positions of individuals within the same household.

Further complexities can also be noted by comparing in Figure 1.1 the potential consequences of poverty to some of the causal factors identified. Poor health may result in lower earnings – it may also stem from poverty or a disadvantaged employment position. In terms of policy response, tackling poor health might imply increasing incomes among the poorest, while tackling poverty might imply improving the health of those of working age and, possibly, making it easier for those with health problems to work, as suggested, for example, by the Green Paper on Welfare Reform (DWP, 2006a).

A particular complexity is indicated by the dotted arrow leading from one set of potential causes of low earnings/non-employment to the role of family structure. It is important to recognise that living arrangements are not independent of individual characteristics or poverty. Those with limited earning capacity (and no independent means) may be led to cohabit with others. This may introduce benefits of sharing (economies of scale) but may put pressure on overall household income and potentially lead to overcrowding. Similarly, the experience of racism may both limit job opportunities, but may also lead to preferences for living with or in close proximity to other family members (Harrison, 2003), with potential impacts on experience of poverty and future opportunities. Just as poverty is experienced at the individual level but tends to stem from what is going on at the household level, so causes of poverty stem from the interconnectedness of households and individuals, and from how these interconnections do or do not translate into poverty. Households may also be connected to each other through kinship or norms of obligation or reciprocity to each other. The interpretation of the household as a distinct unit for income and expenditure may thus be an oversimplification.

This issue of the interconnection of household, individual and society or social structures is an important consideration when looking at the relationship between poverty and ethnicity. However, when investigating the causes of earnings and employment disadvantage, much of the literature is highly individualised. Characteristics and preferences, rather than social structures or the complex interplay between individuals, families and structures tend to be seen as the only necessary elements to understanding ethnic difference. However, the construction of 'preferences' in a relational context is critical. People may 'prefer' to undertake jobs where they are not subject to racism, they also may 'prefer' to undertake the job they get rather than one that was denied them. To what extent such uses of the idea of preference is meaningful is, however, highly debatable. This focus on individualised outcomes is also a disciplinary one: it is a dominant feature of the economics literature on ethnicity and migration. And in the process of conducting the review it became clear how relatively little 'conversation' there was between different disciplines in attempting to answer fundamentally similar questions.

Disciplinary differences in perspective mean that bringing them together to consider causes of poverty requires taking sufficient account of the perspectives from which they are constructed. This is necessary to provide an accurate account, but it does not necessarily mean endorsing that perspective. For example, investigations in much of the health-related literature start from an assumption of self-evident ethnic differences, which are then examined for their effects on outcomes, rather than, say, looking for a common cause. Alternatively, in some of the sociological or social policy literature, the interpretation of *every* inequality found among ethnic groups is regarded as evidence of systematic disadvantaging by the state. By contrast, in much of the economics literature, the explanation of ethnic difference is located in individual characteristics. As long as all relevant characteristics can be identified, the assumption is, the differences will disappear.

In moving on to consider causes of poverty in Part Three of this book, for ease of coverage, I do take a number of the factors identified as contributing distinctly to differences in poverty risks. Thus, qualifications and other aspects of 'human capital' are considered in detail; and family structure is treated separately from benefit eligibility and take-up. Nevertheless, it is important to bear in mind that (a) these distinctions are somewhat artificial; (b) they do not presuppose a particular understanding of the relationship between ethnicity and outcomes; and (c) for their impact to be fully understood they have to be related to wider societal processes.

Before I move on to either the evidence of poverty or discussion of its causes, I consider, in the next two chapters, issues of definition and measurement, starting with a consideration of what we understand by ethnicity and how it is interpreted for the purposes of this book.

Notes

[1] Project website can be found at www.iser.essex.ac.uk/home/lplatt

[2] The ethnic group questions from both the 1991 and 2001 Census are discussed further in Chapter Two and are outlined in Note 1 of that chapter.

[3] In this review 'Britain' is used to refer to the three countries: England, Wales and Scotland; and 'the UK' is used to refer to those countries plus Northern Ireland.

Part One
Concepts and definitions

TWO

Ethnicity and ethnic groups

Ethnicity is usually taken to represent a self-claimed identity linked to a perception of some combination of common history, origins or customs and possibly religion shared with those of the same ethnicity. There is an extensive literature discussing the meaning and use of the terminology of ethnicity and ethnic group, and both its distinctiveness from and overlap with the terminology of 'race' and of national identity. See, for example, Smith (1991), Ratcliffe (1994), Banton (1997, 1998), Cornell and Hartmann (1998) and Mason (2000). Here, I do not attempt to consider these issues in detail, but simply to outline some core points of concern to this review.

An ethnic group is, theoretically, one where the association with both a particular origin and specific customs is adopted by people themselves to establish a shared identity. Weber (1978) defined an ethnic group in the following terms:

> We shall call 'ethnic groups' those human groups that entertain a subjective belief in their common descent because of similarities of physical type or of customs or both, or because of memories of colonization and migration; this belief must be important for the propagation of group formation; conversely, it does not matter whether or not an objective blood relationship exists. (Weber, 1978, p 389)

The main elements of this definition, the notion of shared history and belonging and the fact that connections do not have to be based in objective fact (see also Anderson, 1991), have been subsequently taken up in more recent discussions of the meaning of ethnicity and ethnic group. However, in subsequent work the importance of shared religion as frequently a core element in ethnic identification has sometimes been highlighted. (See the discussion in Cornell and Hartmann, 1998.)

Nevertheless, despite the influence of his definition, Weber is at pains to point out that the clusters of characteristics mobilised around the idea of an ethnic group (as around the idea of the nation) will vary with each given situation: 'the concept of the 'ethnic group' ... dissolves if we define our terms exactly' (Weber, 1978, p 395). That is, the way and the fact that an 'ethnic group' comes into being cannot be predicted, and neither can the factors that create or sustain an ethnic group be generalised from one situation to another. This contingent and fluid nature of ethnicity is often overlooked in – or presents a problem for – analyses of ethnic group differences. Indeed, the promise of ethnicity in suggesting that flexible cultural bonds, rather than fixed hereditary characteristics, are at the heart of ethnic difference can instead risk leading to a rigid and essentialist view of culture. In simplistic accounts, 'culture' can also appear to become the preserve of 'the other', an additional characteristic of minority ethnic groups, rather than the means through and in which all people live, which is inherently relational and which gives meaning to the world and to all social relations (Geertz, 1993). This is the case with some of the literature reviewed here. In reporting the literature it is impossible to avoid such accounts but they are treated with necessary caution.

Ethnic groups can also be argued to become 'groups', at least in part, through mobilisation and through the establishment of boundaries – either by those within the group or those outside the group (Barth, 1969). Thus, ethnic groups are constructed through processes of recognition, both self-recognition and recognition by others; and ethnic groups include the various 'White' populations of the UK. This point is often made, but is equally often ignored in practice (Bhavnani et al, 2005). On the other hand, whiteness itself has been historically subject to a process of identification with 'European' and thereby to act as an organising principle for inclusion and exclusion of individuals, a process which Bonnett (2000) has identified with the project of modernity itself. And colour has now been a longstanding and crucial element in how ethnic groups are conceived, responded to and subjected to processes of inclusion and exclusion in the UK (Berthoud, 1998a; Goulbourne, 1998).

Expressed or chosen identity is often not captured in sources of information about minority ethnic groups: questions are not left open and the options offered indicate that in seeking information on ethnic origin surveys and censuses are attempting to capture something about the 'non-White' population of the UK aggregated to reflect a number of common aspects of 'identity' such as immigration history, forebears' nationality, region of origin, religion and so on. How to adequately represent self-expressed identities while allowing for 'objective indicators' to measure inequalities across groups is a subject of ongoing debate (Modood et al, 2002). Systems of categorisation have been continually contested and critiqued – even among those who support the collection of 'ethnicity data' (Butt et al, 1991; Simpson, 2005). Others, of course, reject any attempt at 'racialised' categorisation (Gilroy, 2000).

The 1991 Census question is one prominent and much discussed case that attempted to seek self-identification while creating an ethnically differentiated measure of Britain's population with a particular focus on 'visible' minority ethnic groups. The nature of, and problems with, the question has been extensively considered in various discussions (Bulmer, 1996; Coleman and Salt, 1996b; Karn et al, 1997), with Ratcliffe (1996b) going so far as to assert that the one thing the question does not measure is ethnicity. Howard (2006) stresses the political nature of ethnic group designations and their inclusion in Census questions. The, often unspoken assumption is that what constitutes the 'non-White' population is self-evident and that its interest is equally self-evident (Mason, 2000). In this process, 'ethnic group' becomes racialised and identified with minority ethnicity (Ballard, 1996a) and White UK-born becomes ever more normalised by its exclusion from ethnicity (Bhavnani et al, 2005). The potential that is offered by the increasing range and longstanding existence of ethnic classifications for understanding and monitoring equality also, therefore, presents a potential danger in relation to 'essentialising' groups (Bonnett and Carrington, 2000); and by encouraging explanations of differences in outcomes to be sought in ethnic differences they may promote 'cultural' or racialised accounts over structural ones and thus even potentially reinforce disadvantage (Nazroo, 2003).

Attachment to fixed categories can also mean that understandings of ethnicity are not allowed to develop or to respond to changes in identification or changes in the ethnic group composition of the UK. The 1991 Census question *was* changed for the 2001 Census,[1] despite the impact on comparability that that would have (ONS, 2003); and government sources, such as the Labour Force Survey, changed over to the new question at the same point (Smith, 2002). The new question was altered to acknowledge that those of 'Mixed' heritage had not felt the previous classification catered for them and that the number of people who might wish to claim such a heritage was increasing (Aspinall, 2001). (For a discussion of the 'Mixed' groups, see Bradford, 2006.) It also included a new 'Irish' category to enable the analysis of those who perceived themselves as Irish (Walls, 2001; Howard, 2006). In addition, the way the question was asked also changed, so that it placed more emphasis on 'cultural' background and less on heritage or ancestry (Platt et al, 2005). Furthermore, in 2001, an ethnic group question was asked in Northern Ireland, where it hadn't been previously, and the question and output differed in Scotland from that used in England and Wales.

Ethnicity and ethnic group membership may be a property of all people; they are, however, situational (Mason, 2003a) and relational (Alam and Husband, 2006); and although we tend to think of ethnicity as a fixed characteristic, its salience and what is taken to be one's own ethnic identity or primary identity will vary with context. Moreover, ethnic identification will also change over time in some cases, both as a result of what opportunities for self-classification are offered but also given inherent fluidity in ethnic identification (Platt et al, 2005).

Nevertheless, despite the acknowledgement of some changes both in the population and in perceptions of ethnicity implied by the shift in categories between 1991 and 2001, there remain questions about the extent to which existing categories are adequate (Kyambi, 2005), the assumptions underlying them, and the extent to which they construct artificial or meaningless bounds round disparate sets of individuals. Categorisation may be an important tool for monitoring disadvantage and facilitating anti-discrimination legislation (www.cre. gov.uk/duty/ethnicmonitoring.html). However, the process of monitoring may effectively impose particular identifications on individuals – thus undermining the 'owned' aspect of identity. Moreover, it may be felt that ethnic group categories only partially capture the forms of difference between population subgroups that they are intended or expected to represent.

In reviewing the research around poverty and ethnicity, it is possible to observe a number of analytical strategies used in identifying the core subject for research. These vary with the perception of what a group is intended to represent (for example source of identity, potential source of disadvantage, marker of difference); with the (explicit or implicit) aim of the research (for example to highlight inequality or to reveal diversity), and with the underlying view of the world, which ranges at the extremes from total individualism to a focus on disembodied structures to the exclusion of individual agency.

Thus, some research, and often that which seeks to identify differences purely in terms of individual characteristics, stresses the fact of immigration as the key point of differentiation (see, for example, Dustmann and Fabbri, 2005a). Here, interest is in the impact of migration itself on life chances – and the related assumption that because they share the process of migration it is appropriate to join immigrants together – they are linked by more than what separates them. This may seem implausible given the diversity in backgrounds, migration histories, settlement patterns and subsequent trajectories that have been illustrated for the different minority ethnic groups of the UK (Al-Rasheed, 1996; Ballard, 1996b; Chance, 1996; Cheng, 1996; Daley, 1996; Eade et al, 1996; Owen, 1996a, 1996b; Peach, 1996b; Robinson, 1996a). On the other hand, Hickman (2005) has highlighted the importance of understanding Britain's colonial past in relation to commonality of the experience of minorities.

Research may also distinguish immigrants by 'ethnicity' – which can either refer to their particular country of birth (see, for example, Wheatley Price, 2001a), or to their self-identified ethnic group (see, for example, Salt, 1996). Others, however, will use the language of 'ethnicity' to distinguish between British or UK-born 'ethnic groups' and foreign-born 'immigrants'. Other research that retains a focus on the main ethnic group categories will, nevertheless, separate out the British born from the foreign born among the different self-reported ethnicities (see, for example, Heath and McMahon, 2005). Sometimes this will be, implicitly or explicitly, to engage with the literature that stresses immigration as the central feature of difference (see, for example, Blackaby et al, 2005).

Those interested in trends and changes in the composition and origins of immigrants (Kyambi, 2005) and their skill mix (Dustmann et al, 2005) and how that relates to overall changes in society may also be more concerned with immigration and immigration flows (Hatton and Wheatley Price, 2005); as may those wishing to test the impact of migration on local labour markets (Hatton and Tani, 2005; Longhi et al, 2006). In these discussions there is sometimes a distinction between 'British-born', 'settled migrants' and 'new migrants' (Kyambi, 2005). Those concerned with projecting distributions of ethnic groups and other demographic characteristics into the future, for example in considering the impact of an ageing population and pension provision, may well have an interest in recent (and future) flows of immigration (Pensions Commission, 2004).

An interest in new migrants may also be connected to concerns with status, issues of legality and how legislation and perception shape identification and position. Here a particular concern may be the status and marginalisation of particular immigrant groups, illegal immigrants and refugees (or asylum seekers). The particular lack of rights of these groups (Mercorios, 1997) means that they are especially disadvantaged and vulnerable to poverty (Carter, 1996; Fitzpatrick, 2005). Thus, regardless of their 'ethnicity' they could be considered groups worthy of analysis to highlight their disadvantage and of policy attention to ameliorate it (Grenier, 1996) (although this is not the approach taken in the coverage of this review). Those concerned with human rights may pay particular attention to these groups.

For some commentators, religious difference is both potentially the most important element of personal identification (Jacobson, 1997, 1998; Modood, 1997a; Tyrer and Ahmad, 2006) and, it is argued, the most striking indicator of disadvantage and discrimination (Modood, 1992, 1997b; Modood et al, 1994). The gendered nature of discrimination against Muslims has also been highlighted (Tyrer and Ahmad, 2006). There remains, nevertheless, a complex interplay of ethnicity and religion (Alam and Husband, 2006). Some analysis by religion crosses 'ethnic group' boundaries to use religious affiliation as the defining characteristic of groups (Ansavi, 2002); other research uses religion to reveal diversity within ethnic groups (Platt, 2005a) and yet other research shows diversity in outcomes associated with religion by ethnic group (Brown, M.S., 2000; Peach, 2006). The intersection of religion and ethnicity for particular groups has also been focused on to enrich our understanding of the strategic use of religion against 'cultural' claims as well as the inseparability of the two elements of identification (Brah and Shaw, 1992; Alam and Husband, 2006). Recent analysis of the 2001 Census provides an overview of patterns in population, labour market and family structure by ethno-religious groups, aiding our understanding of the overlaps and distinctiveness of these intersections (Dobbs et al, 2006). Nevertheless, despite this expansion of information, there remains much work to be done in developing interpretive strategies for ethno-religious diversity.

An interest in the nature of identification has also resulted in consideration of the extent to which people identify with particular nationalities or with 'Britishness' (Parekh, 2000). Of those participating in a series of focus groups conducted by Ethnos who were from different ethnic groups living in the three countries of Britain, it was the minority ethnic participants resident in England who identified most strongly as British (Ethnos, 2005). For those in Scotland and Wales, whether from the White majority or from a minority ethnic group, being Welsh or Scottish was a stronger source of identification than being British, whereas 'Englishness' was associated with being White by minority ethnic group participants. Kim (2005) further explored what the meaning of and any challenges to the notion of 'Britishness' might be, coming from both devolution and a strong European agenda; while Hussain and Bagguley (2005) explored citizenship as identity and how it varies between first- and second-generation Pakistanis.

Having said that, the majority of relevant research relating to the review uses some form of ethnic group categorisation either as the main or as a subsidiary distinction, typically using either the 1991 or 2001 Census categories. In some cases this involves aggregating ethnic groups into larger categories, depending on the source and the level of the analysis, although where there is the option I have favoured lower levels of aggregation. In addition, a few pieces of research, typically local, qualitative studies are able to examine more specific categories.

In what follows, the findings will adapt to the processes of distinction that were used and the groups that were identified, employing the terms of the original research. But it is important to remember that there are not simply issues of comparability between research using different categories, but the way that populations are broken down and ethnicity conceived of (or subsumed into migrant /non-migrant) is also important in framing the assumptions and objectives of the research itself. Peach (2005, p 179) has claimed that 'The discourse has moved from color to culture, from immigration to minorities, from minorities to gender and religion'; however, these developments in discourse are not apparent in all the research considered in this book.

As an overview of the prevalence of different groups and categories, Table 2.1 provides the ethnic group populations of the four countries of the UK, and for the UK overall. It shows both the differences in shares of minority ethnic groups and the different distributions of minority ethnic groups across the four countries. It also shows the differences in categories across the countries, with the largest variation being in the coding of White groups, although Scotland and Northern Ireland also only have one general Mixed category. The table illustrates the extent to which (White) people born in England, Scotland, Wales or Northern Ireland comprise larger or smaller minority ethnic groups when resident in one of the other countries of the UK. As it makes clear, most of the UK's minority ethnic groups live in England. This is not simply due to the fact that most of the UK population lives in England, as the minority ethnic group share of the population of England is greater than that for the other countries. Only 2% of the population of Wales is from one of the 2001 Census minority ethnic groups, and less than 1% of the population of Northern Ireland. Or, to put it another way, as the final row of the table shows, Wales has around 5% of the UK population but only 1.3% of its non-White minority population.[2] Moreover, within countries there is a great deal of variation in distribution. For example, over 45% of the UK's minority ethnic groups live in London, and the majority of Wales' minority ethnic groups live in Cardiff (National Statistics, 2004a). The distribution of minority ethnic groups by region is illustrated in Figure 2.1.

On the other hand, there are different ways of breaking down populations into subgroups that may appear significant or where ascertaining differences may be considered important; and Table 2.2 provides information on religious affiliation from the 2001 Census. It provides the information separately for Britain and for Northern Ireland, and, for the latter, it also provides a breakdown by 'community' background, which is distinguished from own religious affiliation.

Table 2.1: Ethnic group distributions across the UK according to the 2001 Census (%)

Ethnic group	England	Wales	Scotland	Northern Ireland	UK
White British	86.99	95.99			
Scottish			88.09		
White Irish	1.27	0.61	0.98		
Other British			7.38		
Other White	2.66	1.28	1.54		
Irish Traveller				0.10	
WHITE				99.15	92.1
Mixed White and Black Caribbean	0.47	0.2			
Mixed White and Black African	0.16	0.1			
Mixed White and Asian	0.37	0.2			
Mixed Other	0.31	0.1			
MIXED			0.25	0.20	1.2
Indian	2.09	0.28	0.3	0.09	1.8
Pakistani	1.44	0.29	0.63	0.04	1.3
Bangladeshi	0.56	0.19	0.04	0.01	0.5
Other Asian	0.48	0.12	0.12	0.01	0.4
Black Caribbean	1.14	0.09	0.04	0.02	1
Black African	0.97	0.13	0.1	0.03	0.8
Other Black	0.19	0.03	0.02	0.02	0.2
Chinese	0.45	0.22	0.32	0.25	0.4
Other	0.44	0.18	0.19	0.08	0.4
TOTAL (=100%)	49,138,831	2,903,085	5,062,011	1,685,267	58,789,194
Total as a share of UK population	83.58	4.94	8.61	2.87	100
Country's share of non-White minority ethnic population as a share of all non-White minority ethnic population	96.21	1.33	2.19	0.27	100

Sources: 2001 Census, Office for National Statistics, General Register Office for Scotland, Northern Ireland Statistics and Research Agency

Figure 2.1: Distribution of 2001 Census minority ethnic groups by region

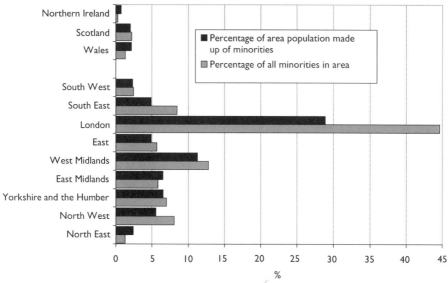

Table 2.2: Religious affiliation in Britain and Northern Ireland, 2001 (%)

	Northern Ireland	Britain
Christian		71.8
Catholic	40.3	
Presbyterian Church in Ireland	20.7	
Church of Ireland	15.3	
Methodist Church in Ireland	3.5	
Other Christian	6.1	
Buddhist		0.3
Hindu		1.0
Jewish		0.5
Muslim		2.8
Sikh		0.6
Any other		0.3
Non-Christian religion	0.3	
None or not stated	13.9	22.2
Community background (NI)		
Catholic	43.8	
Protestant	53.1	
Other	0.4	
None	2.7	

Source: National Statistics (2004b); Northern Ireland Statistics and Research Agency

Table 2.3: Largest ethno-religious groups, 2001 (%)

	Proportion of population	Proportion of ethnic group	Proportion of religious group
White British Christian	66.8	75.7	93.0
White British no religion	13.8	15.7	91.7
White British Jewish	0.4	0.4	84.0
White British Muslim	0.1	0.1	4.0
White British Buddhist	0.1	0.1	34.2
White Irish Christian	1.0	85.7	1.4
White Irish no religion	0.1	6.2	0.5
Other White Christian	1.6	62.9	2.2
Other White no religion	0.4	16.1	2.7
Other White Muslim	0.2	8.3	7.4
Other White Jewish	0.1	2.3	12.4
Mixed Christian	0.6	52.3	0.9
Mixed no religion	0.3	23.3	1.8
Mixed Muslim	0.1	9.7	4.1
Indian Hindu	0.8	44.8	84.4
Indian Sikh	0.5	29.2	91.3
Indian Muslim	0.2	12.6	8.3
Indian Christian	0.1	5.0	0.1
Pakistani Muslim	1.2	91.9	43.2
Bangladeshi Muslim	0.5	92.4	16.5
Other Asian Muslim	0.2	37.5	5.8
Other Asian Hindu	0.1	26.3	11.7
Other Asian Christian	0.1	13.5	0.1
Black Caribbean Christian	0.7	73.7	1.0
Black Caribbean no religion	0.1	11.3	0.7
Black African Christian	0.6	68.8	0.8
Black African Muslim	0.2	20.0	6.1
Chinese no religion	0.2	53.0	1.5
Chinese Christian	0.1	21.1	0.1
Chinese Buddhist	0.1	15.1	24.7
Other ethnic group Christian	0.1	32.8	0.2
Other ethnic group no religion	0.1	14.0	0.4
Other ethnic group Muslim	0.1	26.0	3.8
Other ethnic group Buddhist	0.1	15.3	23.6

Notes: Groups with a population size of less than 30,000 have been excluded from the table. The ethno-religious groups listed account, in total, for nearly 92% of the population.

Source: Adapted from Bosveld and Connolly (2006, table 2.3) (from the 2001 Census for England and Wales and Scotland)

Table 2.3, by contrast, provides information just on Britain, but outlines the intersection between ethnicity and religion – for the largest combinations. It not only describes the religious distributions within the main ethnic groups, but also shows how the different religions are distributed across the population. For example, while 43% of British Muslims are from the Pakistani ethnic group, 8% are Indian and 6% are Black African. And it gives some additional definition to the residual 'other' groups, even as it aggregates the Mixed groups into one category. (For more on the composition of the 'other ethnic group' category, see Gardener and Connolly, 2005.)

The additional area that is relevant to this book is that of current or recent immigrants and those with different immigration statuses. It is possible to think of them in relation to either current entrants or to the stock in the country at any one time, that is, including those who have entered over a period of time but excluding those who have subsequently left. Flows are easier to measure than getting precise information on stocks by status and the numbers in each of the main categories are outlined here. They clearly represent the most recent migrants but will only affect the composition of the immigrant group to the extent that they remain. A large proportion of emigrants are transitory, with nearly half of them leaving again within five years; and others will engage in onward or return migration after longer periods as well (Rendall and Ball, 2004). Staying or leaving is in part related to status and the reason for being resident in the first place. According to the Home Office, in 2003, 299,000 people entered the UK as students (or as their dependants), 121,000 work permit holders and their dependants arrived and 62,300 working holidaymakers and 11,500 seasonal workers were given leave to enter (Dudley et al, 2005). Those admitted as a spouse or fiancé(e) (on a probationary period) constituted 35,200 entrants. The figures do not include those who were given leave to enter as asylum seekers, as they are included in the 'other' category of 190,000 people. However, in, 2004 there were 40,600 asylum applications in the UK (National Statistics, 2006); and in 2003, 54,310 asylum-related grants were made, including family members (Dudley et al, 2005).

Notes

[1] The 1991 Census categories were derived from a tick-box question that offered: White, Black Caribbean, Black African, Black Other, Indian, Pakistani, Bangladeshi, Chinese, Any other ethnic group, with 'please describe' for Black Other and Any other ethnic group. Published output typically divided 'other' responses into 'Other Asian' and 'Other Other'. These categories were the same across England, Scotland and Wales. In 2001 the question for England and Wales took the form 'What is your ethnic group? Choose ONE section from 'A' to 'E', then tick the appropriate box to indicate your cultural background'. 'A' was White and had boxes for British, Irish, Any other White background. 'B' was Mixed and had boxes for White and Black Caribbean, White and Black African, White and Asian, Any other mixed background. 'C' was Asian or Asian British and had boxes for

Indian, Pakistani, Bangladeshi, Any other Asian background. 'D' was Black or Black British and had boxes for Caribbean, African, Any other Black background. 'E' was Chinese or Other ethnic group. Each of the five 'Any other' options invited write-in answers. In Scotland the format was similar, but 'A' included Scottish and Other British in place of British; there were no sub-options for 'B'; 'C' included Chinese; and 'D', therefore just consisted of Any other ethnic group. Northern Ireland did not have an ethnic group question in 1991. In 2001 the ethnic group question took the form 'To which of these ethnic groups do you consider you belong?'. Tick-box options were: White, Chinese, Irish Traveller, Indian, Pakistani, Bangladeshi, Black Caribbean, Black African, Black Other, Mixed and Any other, with write-in options for the two 'other' categories.

[2] Given the different ways of measuring White minority groups across the four countries it was not possible to include White minority groups in this calculation.

THREE

Poverty and deprivation

In order to assess the prevalence of poverty for ethnic groups and the differences between groups, it is necessary to consider what exactly is meant by poverty. Despite the apparently self-evident nature of poverty, both conceptualisation and measurement are much debated. Here I briefly rehearse the key points of these debates, which I have covered in more detail elsewhere (Platt, 2002, 2006b); see also Lister (2004).

Income poverty

Poverty has long been considered as best identified by lack of income to ensure a viable living standard. Income (the money that comes in) is assumed to have a direct connection with standard of living. This is generally speaking a not unreasonable assumption to make. People may use debt to spend above their incomes or they may reduce the benefit they get from income by saving. But extensive use of debt to maintain living standards is not very viable in the long term (indeed servicing debt, particularly if at high rates of interest, is likely to further decrease living standards for those on a low income), and saving at low income levels is neither very plausible, nor supported by the evidence, as is shown in Chapter Four.[1]

Income as a measure of poverty also has the advantage of transparency: it is clear what is being measured; and it does not require, as deprivation measures do, that some decision is made about what constitutes deprivation. Furthermore, this also means it is flexible, in that it does not require information about how people spend their money nor expectations that they should spend it in a particular way. This makes it particularly suitable to measure ethnic group differences, where definition on the basis of 'essentials' may be found to be inadequate if what constitutes an 'essential' is ethnically specific. There still remains, however, the possibility that different levels of income cannot enable the same level of satisfaction of needs, because of differences in the costs of those needs.

An additional problem with income measures is that they assume by default that there is equal sharing of income within the household. This is unlikely to be accurate, and instead there has been substantial attention drawn to issues of gender within the household. Income distribution is likely to be related to control of income, but even when women have control they may prioritise the needs of members of the household other than themselves. Control in a low-income household may simply represent a burden of responsibility for managing scarce resources (Morris and Ruane, 1989). Children may also be protected in otherwise poor households with adults going without to support them (Middleton and

Ashworth, 1995; Gordon et al, 2000); although Gregg et al (1999) found that expenditure on children mirrored income and that therefore poverty was having a serious impact on children. (Conversely, Gregg et al, 2005, showed that as low-income-family incomes increased, spending on children also increased.)

Income is used as a standard measure of low income in the government's Households Below Average Income (HBAI) statistics, produced annually. It is also one of the key measures used in the *Opportunity for All* annual reports monitoring poverty and indicators of life chances (DWP, 2006b). The measure of income used is those living with equivalised household incomes below 60% of the contemporary median. Equivalisation refers to the fact that total household incomes are adjusted by the number of people in them. Thus, for example, a one-person household on £300 per week is deemed better off than a two-person household on £300 per week. The median refers to the mid-point of the distribution of equivalised incomes. Additional poverty measures used in *Opportunity for All* include a measure of poverty over time. 'Persistent poverty' is defined as being below 60% of the median for three years out of four (with an alternative measure of below 70% of the median for three years out of four). This acknowledges the fact that poverty that is long term is more problematic – for both the individual and society – than poverty that is transient.

After a process of consultation on its aim to eliminate child poverty, the government decided that deprivation measures should constitute, alongside income measures, one of the ways in which progress in eradicating child poverty is evaluated. Deprivation measures were subsequently incorporated into the Family Resources Survey from 2004, alongside additional measures on debt (DWP, 2003), and thus provide the potential for providing ethnic group breakdowns of deprivation. They have not been considered in the most recent report on the Family Resources Survey (DWP, 2006c), and separate analysis had not yet been completed at the time of writing this book. Nevertheless, there is a small amount of research evidence on ethnicity and deprivation; and I go on to discuss deprivation definitions of poverty next.

Deprivation

It has been argued that as income is a proxy for poverty and poverty is concerned with having a particularly low standard of living, we should try to measure that standard of living directly; and that we should do this through looking at what people lack that they might be expected to need, thus examining the extent to which they are deprived. While this sounds reasonable, it raises questions of which aspects of life should be measured to ascertain if people are deprived or not. In some cases necessaries that people should not be without have been defined through asking the population at large to vote on what is 'necessary' (Mack and Lansley, 1985; Gordon and Pantazis, 1997; Gordon et al, 2000; Pantazis et al, 2006). In other cases a more top-down approach is used depending either on the researcher's judgement or on what is available within the source being used (Townsend, 1979; Nolan and Whelan, 1996).

Areas that tend to be covered when examining deprivation, either together or separately, are:

- housing problems such as damp, leakages or lack of central heating;
- lack of an outdoor coat or shoes;
- household repair;
- regular meals and sometimes the content of those meals;
- some forms of social activity, such as having friends round;
- sometimes avoidance of debt or the ability to save.

See, for example, the list in Annex A of *Measuring Child Poverty* (DWP, 2003). This list compares closely with those asked, for example, in the British Household Panel Survey, although in the former case there is also an additional set relating specifically to children, which compares with those used in the Poverty and Social Exclusion Survey (Gordon et al, 2000).

Housing deprivation is sometimes treated as an issue to be tackled in its own right (Somerville and Steele, 2002). But it can also be treated as an element (or indicator) in an index of deprivation (Pantazis et al, 2006). Or it can be treated as a dimension of deprivation (Nolan and Whelan, 1996).

Subjective measures

Poverty can be measured not simply in terms of what people have or lack, either in income or 'necessities', but also in terms of how they are feeling about their finances. Thus, some surveys, such as the British Household Panel Survey, include questions about perceptions of financial situation with options for answers ranging from 'living comfortably' to 'finding it very difficult'. Platt (2006b) provides a summary of responses to this question in 2001. Feelings of financial stress could be considered either a measure of poverty or as a consequence of insufficient income. Some objections to subjective measures arise because feelings of financial stress or worry are not necessarily very closely related to income. However, they provide an additional useful 'take' on the experience of poverty, as well as on its potential consequences. There is little coverage of such subjective views on poverty by ethnic group, although there were questions about money worries and financial management in the Fourth National Survey of Ethnic Minorities (Berthoud, 1997); but further work in this area could enhance our understanding of the meaning of poverty and coping responses among different ethnic groups.

Social exclusion and participation

Townsend (1979) famously linked poverty with participation in society. The issue of participation also relates to the extent to which the outcomes that I have considered as consequences of poverty in Figure 1.1 can be used as indicators of poverty. For example, does lack of social activity constitute poverty or is it a consequence of poverty? Given the complexity of identifying general measures of participation, and the particular potential difficulty when comparing across groups who may have different patterns of social activity, or where preferences may differ starkly across generations of one group but not of another, I have not attempted to include such participatory indicators in this review. Nevertheless, the extent to which members of different ethnic groups have opportunities for social, cultural and political participation over and above income, and the extent to which this represents deprivation or poverty remain important issues for research (Platt, 2006a).

The idea of participation is also implicated in definitions of social exclusion (Hills et al, 2002). By nature of being multifaceted, the notion of social exclusion can capture something of the complexity in the experience of poverty among minority ethnic groups and its relationship to other forms of marginalisation. However, its very complexity means that social exclusion is both hard to measure and difficult to distinguish from its potential causes. Indeed the cycles implicit in social exclusion and the connections between causes and effects are one of its key features.[2] A further problem with social exclusion in the context of this review is that ethnicity can begin to be used as an indicator of exclusion rather than as a potential source of variation in the distribution of social exclusion. It has been argued that by virtue of their experiences of disadvantage and exclusion through racism and discrimination, minority ethnic groups are or tend to be socially excluded. Certain minority groups are thus defined as vulnerable in relation to the (former) Social Exclusion Unit's agenda (ODPM, 2004a). However, this risks seeing minority ethnicity as a measure – or source – in its own right of disadvantage, rather than assessing the extent to which various forms of disadvantage are associated more or less with particular ethnicities. Thus, the overlap between social exclusion, ethnicity, area deprivation and poverty remains a potentially confusing one.

Social exclusion is defined both as a feature of areas and as a property of individuals. But this then raises the question of what the relationship between individual and area deprivation is. The relationship between individual poverty or social exclusion and deprived neighbourhoods is one that is susceptible to investigation in its own right. The neighbourhood effects literature starts from the premise that there may be additional effects of living in a deprived location over and above the influence of the circumstances of the individual or household. For example, Buck (2001) has explored this question empirically. Rather than assume that those who live in 'socially excluded areas' are themselves socially excluded, it seems more appropriate to investigate the effect of neighbourhood on individuals and whether there is any variation in such effects by ethnic group. Otherwise, there is the danger that the concentration of certain minority ethnic groups in deprived areas will be used to stand in for their own deprivation and will hinder analysis of the extent to which areas are experienced differently by those from different ethnic groups, including in the availability of different forms of social engagement and cultural and political participation. I consider some of these issues further when exploring the role of location in Chapter Five; but because of these various problems of circularity in examining social exclusion and ethnicity, I do not consider it in the description of poverty rates and ethnic variations in Chapter Four .

Regional issues

Poverty rates obviously vary across the UK. People living in some areas will experience much higher rates of poverty than those living in other areas. Although these risks may be independent of their ethnicity, the dominance of particular ethnic or national groups in such areas will mean that they become by virtue of their location more at risk of poverty. Thus, the high levels of poverty in Northern Ireland and in parts of Wales have implications for the poverty risks of (Northern) Irish and Welsh people in the UK. Moreover, while the concentration of certain minority ethnic groups in deprived areas is a feature of their geographical distribution (Dorsett, 1998; Dorling, 2005), there are also predominantly White areas that also experience high levels of poverty, for example parts of the North East of England. There is also diversity in poverty within regions and countries (some areas of Wales are much poorer than others and Glasgow has much more unemployment than the rest of Scotland, for example) and within poor areas. The Indices of Multiple Deprivation show, at small area levels, the distribution of multiple deprivation across England, Wales, Scotland and Northern Ireland (ODPM, 2004b; http://new.wales.gov.uk/topics/statistics/theme/wimd2005/?lang=en; www.scotland.gov.uk/Topics/Statistics/SIMD/Overview; www.nisra.gov.uk/whatsnew/dep/dep_2005.html; Northern Ireland Statistics & Research Agency, 2005). These reveal the great diversity between areas in terms of deprivation within the countries of the UK. And even with a very poor area, the risks of poverty, even if they are high for everyone, can nevertheless vary substantially between groups, as a study of Newham in East London has shown (Platt, 2003a).

A related issue is the situation of national minority ethnic groups within the other countries. There is little information on the situation of, say, Welsh people in Scotland – as opposed to risks of poverty of those living in Wales compared to those living in Scotland, although a recent article drew attention to the particular minority experience of English people in Scotland (McIntosh et al, 2004). With the exception of the rather different case of the experience of those of Irish background living in Britain, we have little data or analysis on those from one country of the UK living as minorities in one of the other countries, (although for Other British people living in Scotland see Scottish Executive, 2004.)

Poverty and inequality

Poverty and inequality have sometimes been conflated (see the discussion in Platt, 2006c). Even though they are conceptually distinct, high rates of inequality are often accompanied by high rates of poverty, although this is not a necessary consequence. Inequality is of concern to this study on two grounds. First, that it is inequalities in the experience of poverty that may make the situation of particular groups of especial concern. Policy may wish to tackle the fact that those from certain ethnic groups are much more likely to be in poverty than others. On the other hand, others may be concerned with poverty wherever it appears or is experienced. Inequality is also relevant in relation to this study in that it is the inequality in the position of certain groups within society that can lead to income inequality. Moreover, inequality in itself has been associated at an aggregate level with the poor health outcomes often associated with poverty (Wilkinson, 1996, 2005). Inequality in access to relevant services may also constitute obstacles to moves out of poverty (Netto, 2006).

Notes

[1] Although those on very precarious incomes may achieve some stability by payment into 'clubs', which could be considered a form of saving, or insurance.

[2] The Social Exclusion Unit website defined social exclusion in the following terms: 'Social exclusion is what happens when people or places suffer from a series of problems such as unemployment, discrimination, poor skills, low incomes, poor housing, high crime, ill health and family breakdown. When such problems combine they can create a vicious cycle. Social exclusion can happen as a result of problems that face one person in their life. But it can also start from birth. Being born into poverty or to parents with low skills still has a major influence on life chances' (http://archive.cabinetoffice.gov.uk/seu/).

Part Two
The facts of poverty

FOUR

Poverty and ethnicity: the evidence

This chapter reviews available literature on poverty prevalence in relation to the groups and poverty measures identified in the previous two chapters. It does not attempt to explain or account for the differences or analyse the different contributory factors – that is left to Chapters Five, Six and Seven in Part Three.

Going back to the model presented in Figure 1.1 in Chapter One, this chapter covers poverty in relation to overall household income, but also investigates what is known about the sources of income in terms of earnings, savings and assets, and benefit income and how those sources vary with ethnicity. Moreover, it also considers those factors that influence the extent to which a given income translates into poverty, those either side of the arrow linking household income and poverty in Figure 1.1: the demands on income and the severity or the duration. It also considers evidence on other measures of poverty, such as deprivation and subjective measures.

Income poverty and composition of income

The most recent direct data on income poverty for the UK can be found in the annual Households Below Average Income (HBAI) series derived from the Family Resources Survey. There are limitations to the tables in these sources, and they employ a relatively high aggregation of minority ethnic groups, in order to ensure robustness of results. However, in the absence of detailed analysis of income and ethnicity since Berthoud's (1998b) study of incomes, income distributions, inequality and sources of income using the Family Resources Survey pooled from the mid 1990s, the HBAI analysis provides the default for contemporary description of variations in poverty rates. Re-analysis of Households Below Average Income statistics allows some refining of this information and the smoothing of it across years and the tables below draw on such re-analysis rather than simply reporting the annually published data. However, the results are consistent with the published series. The poverty definition used in the following tables is those below 60% of median equivalent income, as discussed above. HBAI provides sets of figures before housing costs are taken into account and ones for after housing costs are taken into account. Arguments can be made in favour of either (Platt, 2002), and in Tables 4.1, 4.2 and 4.3 both are provided. With before housing costs estimates, poverty estimates are based on total incomes, rather than on incomes after expenditure on housing has been subtracted. These estimates do not take account of the fact that high housing costs may represent a constraint (for example, as a result of living in a high housing costs area), rather than a reflection of an enhanced quality of life through greater spending on housing. On the other hand, avoiding this problem by using after housing costs measures, which only consider income subsequent to the payment of housing costs, alters the income distribution and raises apparent poverty rates by subtracting housing costs before calculating poverty. Therefore, the inclusion of both sets of estimates allows a comprehensive consideration of both rates and the ways these differ between groups and by household or individual characteristics.

Tables 4.1 and 4.2 show the poverty rates using these definitions by ethnic group, drawing on rolling averages from pooled data for the years 2002/03-2004/05, and for all individuals, children, working-age adults and pensioners respectively. Table 4.1 shows the rates without excluding housing costs and Table 4.2 shows the rates after housing costs have been excluded. Note that the relative position of pensions compared with others appears to be particularly sensitive to the inclusion or exclusion of housing costs. The magnitude of the differences in poverty rates is striking, as is the fact that all minority groups are relatively worse off than those in White groups. And despite the conventional view (and certain evidence, described below) of Indian and Chinese success, individuals from these groups have poverty rates that are 10% higher than those for individuals from White groups, and are comparable with those for individuals from Black groups. However, what really stands out is the poverty risks for Pakistanis and Bangladeshis. Over half of them are in poverty rising to over three fifths of children from these groups. And even

Table 4.1: Poverty rates by ethnic group, 2002/03-2004/05, Britain, calculated before housing costs (%)

Ethnic group	All individuals	Children	Working-age adults	Pensioners
White	15	18	13	21
Mixed	20	25	17	32
Indian	25	28	23	30
Pakistani or Bangladeshi	52	58	48	48
Black or Black British	26	30	23	29
– of which				
Black Caribbean	23	25	21	29
Black non-Caribbean	29	35	25	31
Chinese or Other	26	33	23	21
All	17	20	14	21

Notes: Figures have been calculated from three-year rolling averages for the financial years 2002/03, 2003/04 and 2004/05, and relate to the whole of Britain. Ethnic group is measured at the level of the household and on the basis of the ethnicity of the household reference person. The poverty threshold is calculated as 60% of median equivalised income.
Source: Households Below Average Income data

Table 4.2: Poverty rates by ethnic group, 2002/03-2004/05, Britain, calculated after housing costs (%)

Ethnic group	All individuals	Children	Working-age adults	Pensioners
White	19	25	17	19
Mixed	32	40	28	36
Indian	28	32	25	30
Pakistani or Bangladeshi	59	65	55	48
Black or Black British	38	46	35	27
– of which				
Black Caribbean	30	37	28	26
Black non-Caribbean	46	54	41	31
Chinese or Other	37	44	36	26
All	39	48	46	31

Notes: Figures have been calculated from three year rolling averages for the financial years 2002/03, 2003/04 and 2004/05, and relate to the whole of Britain. Ethnic group is measured at the level of the household and on the basis of the ethnicity of the household reference person. The poverty threshold is calculated as 60% of median equivalised income.
Source: Households Below Average Income data, from the *Family Sources Survey*

working age adults from these groups have an almost 50% risk of poverty, rising to 55% if the after housing costs measure is used.

Table 4.3 provides more detailed breakdowns of child poverty rates specifically, providing in the same table both before and after housing costs estimates together. It also illustrates the risks for households with children compared with the risks for children, to make the simple point that it is the poverty of households that children are living in that results in their poverty rates. Poor households with larger numbers of children will thus result in higher child poverty rates. It shows the extremely high rates of poverty among children in Bangladeshi households when they are disaggregated from the Pakistani group. But it also makes clear how Black African children also face very high risks of poverty.

These descriptive poverty figures are broadly consistent with earlier research that has examined income and ethnicity in more depth. But they tend to invite further analysis along the lines of this earlier research. Berthoud (1998b) investigated pooled data from the Family Resources Survey for 1994/95 and 1995/96 to investigate income differences by ethnicity. He compared the incomes of different types of families – working families, non-working families under the age of 60 and pensioner families – by ethnic group and found that those from Indian, Caribbean, Pakistani and Bangladeshi groups had less income left over ('available income') than their White counterparts after their 'basic needs' had been taken into account. The results illustrated an emphatic difference between the incomes of working Pakistani and Bangladeshi families and the incomes of

Table 4.3: Child poverty rates and rates of poverty among children by ethnic group, 2002/03-2004/05, Britain, before and after housing costs (%)

	Child poverty rates		Households with children rates	
	Before housing costs	After housing costs	*Before housing costs*	After housing costs
White groups	*18*	25	*16*	24
Black Caribbean	*28*	37	*24*	37
Black African	*36*	56	*30*	51
Indian	*28*	32	*25*	29
Pakistani	*56*	60	*51*	56
Bangladeshi	*62*	74	*53*	66

Notes: Figures have been calculated from three-year rolling averages for the financial years 2002/03, 2003/04 and 2004/05, and relate to the whole of Britain. Proportions are based on population-weighted data. Ethnic group is measured at the level of the household and on the basis of the ethnicity of the household reference person. Those living in households where the reference person is of an ethnicity other than those illustrated – or of mixed ethnicity – have been excluded from this discussion due to small sample sizes for individual categories. The poverty threshold is calculated as 60% of median equivalised income.

Source: Households below Average Income data, DWP

working families from all other groups. But even when not taking account of family type, there were large differentials in available income by ethnic group. The relative disadvantage of Caribbeans, Africans and, in particular, Pakistanis and Bangladeshis, was still clear.

Using the General Household Survey for 1991-96, Evandrou (2000) explored the poverty of older people and how it varies by ethnicity. She found that among older people patterns for the different populations as a whole were approximately replicated across groups, with White elders having the lowest levels of income poverty followed by Irish, then Black Caribbean, then Indian and up to 60% of Pakistani and Bangladeshi elders in income poverty. Comparable patterns were also found in an analysis of older people from the Fourth National Survey of Ethnic Minorities (Bajekal et al, 2004). This study found that a range of quality of life measures were patterned by ethnicity in similar ways, with Pakistanis worst off, the White majority best off and Indians and Caribbeans in between, with the exception of measures relating to social contact and perception of location (discussed further in Chapter Five), where the pattern was reversed.

Sources of household income

In Figure 1.1, three components of household income were identified – income from employment, from benefits and from assets and savings. Having considered in the previous section what these add up to above for different ethnic groups in terms of income poverty rates, this section breaks down the evidence on variation in income by ethnic group across these three areas.

Income from employment

Income from employment will vary with both the chances of being in employment and the earnings received. In both these areas there are large differences between identified ethnic groups.

There are two ways of thinking about labour market participation. The first is to explore only those who are in employment. The second is to consider those who are economically active, which is those employed plus those unemployed, as these are potential employees, and counter these to the economically inactive, who are not anticipating or actively seeking paid employment. However, the boundaries of unemployment and economic inactivity can be fairly porous. Nevertheless, it is important to register the differences in unemployment rates as they can give valuable information about the obstacles facing different groups and the extent to which they are attached to the labour market even with unpromising opportunities. All three elements of the picture are probably important in understanding labour market position.

Figure 4.1 shows economic activity rates for men and women from different groups according to the Annual Population Survey for 2004. It illustrates the very low economic activity rates among Pakistani and Bangladeshi women, but also the relatively low rates of economic activity among Pakistani and Bangladeshi men, Chinese men and women and Black African women. However, of those economically active not all are in employment; and Figure 4.2 shows unemployment rates from the same source. It illustrates that unemployment rates are generally higher for men than for women, although Pakistani and Indian women are an exception here. As well as the differences in unemployment rates measured at a point in time, Frijters et al (2005) showed that unemployment durations are also longer for men from minority ethnic groups compared to White British men.

The combination of differences in economic activity and differences in unemployment rates among the economically active lead to overall differences in proportions of different groups actually in work. These are illustrated for men and women in Figures 4.3 and 4.4. We can see that men's employment rates range from a low of under 60% among the Chinese to over 80% among the White British. For women the differences are in line with those for men, with White British and White Irish women having the highest rates, followed by those from Black Caribbean, Indian and Mixed groups, followed by Black African and Chinese women, with Pakistani and Bangladeshi women at the bottom, given their very low economic activity rates to start off with.

Figure 4.1: Economic activity rates by sex and ethnic group, 2004

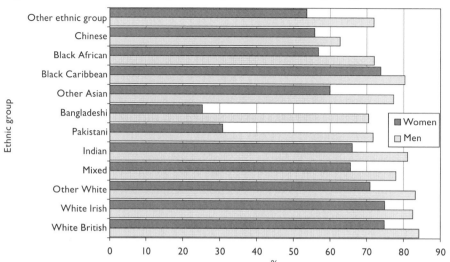

Figure 4.2: Unemployment rates by sex and ethnic group, 2004

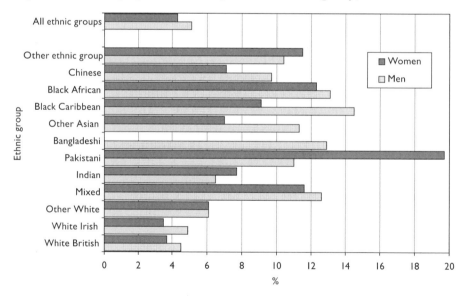

Duffield (2002) explored the employment of women specifically, using the Labour Force Survey for 2002, and found very similar results to those illustrated. These figures do not, however, distinguish the fact that a higher proportion of the White women in employment are in part-time employment. Nor do they consider whether there are differences between groups when caring responsibilities are taken into account. I discuss these points further in Part Three.

Figure 4.3: Employment rates by ethnic group: men, 2004, Britain

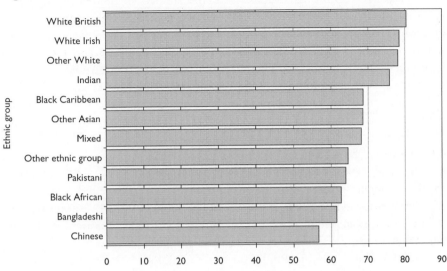

Figure 4.4: Employment rates by ethnic group: women, 2004, Britain

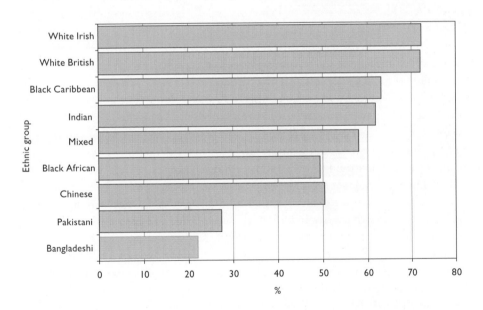

Non-employment can also cluster at the household level, which will have implications for the poverty of the household overall. Walling (2004), analysing the Labour Force Survey for Spring 2004, showed that there was substantial ethnic group variation in the proportion of people of working age living in households that had no one of working age in employment. The lowest rate was for Indians with 10% of those of working age living in such households compared to around

12% of the UK working age overall. Black Africans had the highest risks of living in such a household, with 28% of the working age from this group in such a position. Other groups in which over 20% of working-age adults lived in workless households were Other Black, Chinese, Other, and Pakistani and Bangladeshi (combined). Those with rates over 10% but less than 20% were White groups (combined), Mixed (combined), Other Asian and Black Caribbean.

The low economic activity rates of Pakistani and Bangladeshi women are often taken as evidence of cultural or religious attitudes to women working. However, the fact that those who are economically active have extremely high unemployment rates suggests that it may instead be at least in part a response to limited labour market opportunities (see also Brah and Shaw, 1992). Educated Muslim women's positive attitudes to employment are illustrated in Ahmad et al's (2003) study, while Phillipson et al (2003) showed similarly strong positive attitudes to employment among their sample of first-generation Bangladeshi women. A strategic response to gaining employment is also illustrated by Tackey et al (2006). The women in Phillipson et al's (2003) study expressed constraints in relation to their extensive childcare responsibilities (and sometimes additional caring for adults as well), in relation to lack of English language fluency and to identifying suitable employment opportunities. These results were congruent with those found in a study of Pakistani and Bangladeshi women (Dale, 2002; Dale et al, 2002). In these studies, the younger generation showed much greater engagement with the labour market and positive attitudes towards combining work and family life than the older generation, despite a continued focus on the centrality of the family. However, they faced substantial barriers to employment, with high unemployment rates (see also Tackey et al, 2006). The gendered patterns of change over generations have also been highlighted by Ansari (2002). Dale and colleagues have also explored lifecourse effects on women from different ethnic groups and trends over time in labour market participation. They found that Caribbean women tended to combine children and paid work, whereas Indian and White women were more likely to negotiate the demands of family and work through part-time work, and Pakistani and Bangladeshi women reduced their average labour market participation both on marriage and then further on having children (Dale et al, 2004). But it was also clear that women with certain sets of characteristics and at the same life stage had very similar patterns of economic activity regardless of ethnic group. Thus, women from all groups had very high chances of being economically active if they were young, unmarried and childless and had a degree-level qualification (Dale et al, 2006).

Kyambi (2005), using the Labour Force Survey for 2000-03, showed that there was enormous divergence in employment rates among 'new' immigrants (those who had arrived in the UK after 1990). Some groups had employment rates clearly above the average for those born in the British Isles. These included those born in Australia, Bulgaria, Canada, New Zealand, the Philippines and South Africa, all with employment rates of over 80%. On the other hand, some new immigrants had extremely low employment rates. Those born in Albania, Angola, China, Cyprus, Ethiopia, Iran, Iraq, Korea, Somalia and the former Yugoslavia all had employment rates of under 40%. In some cases, such as those from China, this was largely due to the heavy preponderance of students; while for those from Angola exceptionally high unemployment rates were a major cause of the low employment rates; and in the case of those from Somalia, the majority were economically inactive.

Turning to earnings, recent analysis of earnings data from the Labour Force Survey, 2001–05, shows that even among those who were in paid work, there were some dramatic differences in rates of pay by ethnic group. Table 4.4 shows hourly full-time pay for men and women in the UK from a selection of ethnic groups. Rates of pay were much lower than these full-time rates for part-time workers from all groups, but particularly for Pakistani and Bangladeshi men. Hourly pay becomes income through the number of hours worked, and even among full-time workers there is some variation in the hours worked. Table 4.5 therefore shows the weekly earnings for men and women in full-time work for the same ethnic groups. The substantial differences in these earnings indicate that even those in full-time work may have difficulty escaping poverty, depending of course on the number and earnings of other earners in the household.

For 'new' immigrants there were some striking proportions of those in low pay relative to the British Isles born (Kyambi, 2005). For example, this was true of those born in Bangladesh, China, the former Czechoslovakia, Hong Kong, Iran, Malaysia, Pakistan and Turkey. In most, although not all cases, those with high proportions with low pay also tended to be those new immigrant groups with low employment rates. On the other hand, those born in Australia, Belgium, Canada, Finland, France, Germany, India, Italy, Iran, Japan, the Netherlands, New Zealand, Nigeria, South Africa, Sweden and the US had much higher proportions with high weekly earnings compared to the British Isles born. There are clearly,

Table 4.4: Hourly pay by ethnic group and sex, for those in full-time employment, 2001-05

Ethnic group	Men £	95% confidence intervals £	Women £	95% confidence intervals £
All ethnic groups	11.86 (56,073)	11.79–11.93	9.82 (36,212)	9.76–9.88
White British	11.88 (49,553)	11.81–11.95	9.76 (31,313)	9.69–9.82
Indian	12.57 (880)	11.99–13.16	10.21 (587)	9.71–10.71
Pakistani	9.50 (337)	8.80–10.20	8.38 (134)	7.62–9.14
Bangladeshi	7.17 (104)	6.24–8.09	8.85 (43)	7.64–10.06
Black African	10.48 (288)	9.78–11.18	9.50 (261)	9.00–10.00
Black Caribbean	10.50 (369)	9.89–11.11	10.40 (394)	9.94–10.87

Note: Numbers of individuals in brackets.
Source: Platt (2006d) (from the Labour Force Survey, 2001-05)

Table 4.5: Average weekly pay by ethnic group and sex, for those in full-time employment, 2001-05

Ethnic group	Men £	95% confidence intervals £	Women £	95% confidence intervals £
All ethnic groups	497.89 (56,073)	494.89–500.89	375.80 (36,212)	373.52–378.08
White British	498.57 (49,553)	495.49–501.65	372.79 (31,313)	370.36–375.22
Indian	523.68 (880)	499.81–547.55	396.56 (587)	376.79–416.33
Pakistani	390.24 (337)	361.56–418.92	321.56 (134)	289.20–353.92
Bangladeshi	270.22 (104)	232.04–308.39	324.48 (43)	280.83–368.13
Black African	445.15 (288)	412.43–461.14	372.65 (261)	352.71–392.59
Black Caribbean	436.79 (369)	412.37–475.93	393.71 (394)	376.47–410.95

Note: Numbers of individuals in brackets.
Source: Platt (2006d) (from the Labour Force Survey, 2001-05)

therefore, large polarities in incomes from earnings among recent immigrants, and in some cases, for example those born in Iran, within immigrants from a particular country.

Benefits

Table 4.6 shows for the UK different components of weekly household income according to the ethnic group of the head of the household. It illustrates the shares that come from earned income and those from benefits. Differences in age distributions are evident from the relatively large share of White households' income that is made up of pensions (13%), although by far the largest share still comes from wages and self-employment income (74%). However, as much as 83% of Indian households' income comes from wages and self-employment income. For the other groups, income from work makes up between 73% and 77% of total income, with the exception of Pakistani and Bangladeshi households for whom only 67% of income comes from these sources. Instead, a relatively large share of income for these groups comes from 'other social security benefits', which include Income Support, Housing Benefit and Jobseeker's Allowance among others. Means-tested benefits such as these indicate a lack of alternative resources in terms of both income and savings. They are also much more closely associated with poverty as they are frequently the only source of family income and are paid at rates that frequently put recipients below standard poverty lines. By contrast, non-means-tested benefits can supplement other sources of income and do not necessarily indicate lack of resources.

Table 4.6: Components of total weekly income by ethnic group of head of household, 2002/03-2004/05, UK (%)

Income source	White	Mixed	Indian	Pakistani or Bangladeshi	Black or Black British	Other ethnic group
Wages and salaries	65	68	71	51	68	67
Self-employment income	9	9	12	16	5	10
Investments	2	1	1	1		1
Tax credits	1	2	1	6	2	1
State retirement pension (plus any IS/PC)	6	3	2	3	4	2
Other pensions	7	3	2	1	2	2
Social security disability benefits	2	2	1	2	1	1
Other social security benefits	5	9	5	17	12	8
Other sources	2	4	4	4	4	8

Note: IS = Income Support; PC = Pension Credit.
Source: DWP (2006c, table 3.2)

The Family Resources Survey also tabulates the different means-tested and non-means-tested benefits payable to benefit units according to the ethnic group of the head of the household. Benefit units are the immediate family as assessed for the purpose of calculation of means-tested benefits. That is, the claimant, their partner (if any) and their dependent children (if any). These are illustrated in Table 4.7. The final row shows that use of state support was at roughly similar levels in 2002-05 among White, Pakistani and Bangladeshi and Black or Black British benefit units, while the Mixed, Indian and other groups were lower users of state support. However, the types of state support utilised varied substantially even among those with overall similar rates of use. Part of this is for demographic reasons – thus, we see that the White-headed benefit units were more likely to receive state pensions and the Pakistani and Bangladeshi benefit units were more likely to receive Child Benefit. These contribute to the high totals for both of these groups in relation to non-means-tested benefits. However, Pakistani and Bangladeshi benefit units were also relatively high users of income-related benefits, with 30% of benefit units in receipt of at least one such benefit. Berthoud (1998b), in his study of incomes, also found that Pakistanis and Bangladeshis, the poorest groups in his study, were heavily reliant on means-tested benefits for income (see also Platt, 2003a). By contrast, Table 4.7, shows that, in 2002-5, Indians were the lowest users of income-related benefits with only 14% in receipt.

Table 4.7: Benefit units by state support receipt and ethnic group of head of household, 2002/03-2004/05, UK (%)

	White	Mixed	Indian	Pakistani and Bangladeshi	Black or Black British	Other ethnic groups
Tax credits	10	12	8	19	11	7
Income Support/Minimum Income Guarantee/ Pension Credit	11	13	8	16	15	10
Housing Benefit	12	16	5	12	22	14
Council Tax Benefit	15	18	10	22	24	15
Retirement Pension	26	9	11	7	13	6
Jobseeker's Allowance	2	4	2	5	5	4
Incapacity Benefit	5	3	4	2	3	2
Attendance Allowance	3	1	1	1	1	1
Disability Living Allowance (care component)	5	4	4	4	3	2
Disability Living Allowance (mobility component)	6	4	3	4	3	3
Child Benefit	22	29	25	42	29	21
On any income-related benefit	19	24	14	30	29	20
On any non-income-related benefit	57	43	44	54	47	34
All in receipt of benefit	60	49	47	58	55	41
All in receipt of tax credits	10	12	8	19	11	7
All not in receipt of state support	40	51	53	41	45	58

Source: DWP (2006c adapted from table 3.17)

Platt and Noble's (1999) study of Housing/Council Tax Benefit receipt in Birmingham in 1998 showed that approximately 45% of Bangladeshis were in receipt of either Housing Benefit or Council Tax Benefit and Income Support, and including those on Housing Benefit/Council Tax Benefit who were not on Income Support raised the proportion to over 50%. For Caribbeans, 20% of those on Housing Benefit/Council Tax Benefit were also on Income Support and a further 10% were on Housing Benefit/Council Tax Benefit without Income Support. For Pakistanis, the rates were over 30% with Income Support and over

40% if all those supported by Housing Benefit and/or Council Tax Benefit (including both those in receipt and those not in receipt of Income Support) were considered. These compared with rates in the White population of 14% and 20% respectively.

In their study of 100 middle-aged, 'first-generation' Bangladeshi women living in East London, Phillipson et al (2003) found high levels of benefit use among their sample. Two thirds of the women lived in households in receipt of Income Support, and similar proportions lived in households receiving Housing Benefit or Council Tax Benefit, all means-tested benefits. These women's households also showed high rates of receipt of the non-means-tested benefits Disability Living Allowance or Attendance Allowance (14%), reflecting the number who were married to disabled or chronically sick partners.

Assets and savings

The Family Resources Survey collects detailed information on types of saving and assets. However, in the latest published tables, there is only a breakdown by ethnic group of head of household of type of account, rather than actual amounts (DWP, 2006c). Nevertheless, this still gives some indication of variation in savings and financial assets to contribute to household well-being or to draw on in times of hardship. Table 4.8 provides the information on types of saving and shows that while the vast majority of households across ethnic groups had some sort of bank account, there was substantial variation in those with investments or investment-style accounts. The average portfolio of savings is clearly broadest for the White group and most limited for the Pakistani and Bangladeshi groups; although it is among the Black groups that the highest proportion without any form of account is found. Otherwise the Black groups and other groups tend to fall between the Pakistani and Bangladeshi households on the one hand and the Mixed and Indian households on the other.

In relation to amounts of savings, the 2005 edition of *Social Trends* drew on the Family Resources Survey to provide breakdowns of savings by broad ethnic groupings (ONS, 2005). Wealth is much more concentrated across the population than income, with the wealthiest half of the population owning 92% of marketable wealth (or 93% if housing wealth is excluded). Concentration of wealth across the population is also evident from the savings information illustrated in Table 4.9. This shows that in 2002/03 a third of the population had no savings at all, with 13% having £20,000 or more. But this varied with ethnicity, such that approaching two thirds of the Black and Asian groups had no savings. These broad groupings of ethnic groups are not, however, inherently meaningful, and greater variation would be likely to be observed if it were possible to disaggregate the groups further. (See, for example, the 2001 version of *Social Trends* (ONS, 2001.)

Pensions provide an important form of saving in terms of provision for the future and the welfare of individuals in old age, even if they cannot often be

Table 4.8: Households by type of saving and ethnic group of head of household, 2002/03-2004/05, UK (%)

	White	Mixed	Indian	Pakistani or Bangladeshi	Black or Black British	Other ethnic groups
Current account	90	85	89	86	82	84
Post office account	6	5	3	3	3	3
TESSA	8	3	8	1	2	4
ISA	34	21	25	7	14	20
Other bank/building society account	55	42	42	26	36	38
Stocks and shares/ member of a share club	23	14	20	7	8	14
PEPs	8	4	5	1	2	4
Unit Trusts	5	4	3	1	1	3
Gilts	1	0	0	0	0	0
Premium bonds	24	11	10	2	6	9
National Savings bonds	4	2	2	1	1	1
Company share scheme/profit sharing	5	3	4	1	2	3
Save as you earn	1	1	0	0	0	0
Any type of account	94	91	93	91	88	89

Source: DWP (2006c, adapted from table 5.4)

used to cushion income loss or provide an additional source in terms of high demand prior to retirement. A recent report from the Pensions Commission (2004) broke down pension provision of current pensioners in the UK by three aggregate ethnic groups (White, Asian/Asian British and Black/Black British) and explored the pension arrangements of non-pensioners. It showed that Asian and Black pensioners had on average lower incomes as a result of lower amounts of occupational pension income and investment income, although, again, the level of aggregation of disparate ethnic groups is problematic. Average levels of state pensions and state benefits combined were roughly equal across the groups, but Asian pensioners received less from the Basic State Pension and the State Earnings Related Pension (SERPS) and more from means-tested benefits than White pensioners, with the division for Black pensioners falling between the two.

Ginn and Arber used three pooled years of the Family Resources Survey from 1994/95 to 1996/97 to examine private pension provision among men and women of working age from Bangladeshi, White, Indian, Black, Chinese/Other

Table 4.9: Household savings by ethnic group of head of household, 2002/03, UK

	No savings	Less than £1,500	£1,500 but less than £10,000	£10,000 but less than £20,000	£20,000 or more
White	32	21	26	9	13
Mixed	46	25			
Asian or Asian British	60	15	16	5	5
Black or Black British	63	18	15		
Chinese or Other	50	18	19		
All households	33	20	25	8	13

Source: ONS (2005), table 5.26 (from the Family Resources Survey)

and Pakistani ethnic groups (Ginn and Arber, 2000, 2001). They found that men and women from all minority ethnic groups were less likely to have private pension arrangements than those of the same sex who were White, even after controlling for a range of characteristics. The gap was greatest for the Pakistanis and Bangladeshis, and was largely attributed to more limited access to occupational pensions (Burton, 1997), although the authors did also consider that religious or cultural resistance to investment might be playing a part (such considerations were not found to be significant in Barnes' 2006 study for the Runnymede Trust, however). Poverty risks were found to be greatest for older women across ethnic groups. Qualitative evidence has indicated that lack of knowledge could play a significant role as well (Nesbitt and Neary, 2001). Private pension inequalities between men and women of the same ethnicity were smallest for those from the Black groups, reflecting less interrupted work histories among Black women.

Deprivation

As discussed above, general (national) sources on deprivation have not in the past tended to provide breakdowns by ethnic group. The Family Resources Survey now collects information on deprivation indicators, but this is only a recent development. There are just a few sources on material deprivation that differentiate by ethnicity, although there is a broader literature on ethnic differences in housing conditions, including homelessness, and housing deprivation, which I also touch on here.

Analysis of the Poverty and Social Exclusion Survey contained a breakdown by aggregate 'White' and 'non-White' groups to compare levels of deprivation (Gordon et al, 2000; Pantazis et al, 2006). According to this survey, the 'non-White' group were clearly more deprived according to their measure of deprivation. This was true for children from non-White groups as well (Lloyd, 2006). However, ethnic difference was not a focus of this study; and analysis at such a level of aggregation is not of much value in informing our understanding of deprivation and ethnicity.

Berthoud (1997) explored possession of consumer durables in England and Wales using the Fourth National Survey of Ethnic Minorities. He found that Caribbeans, Indians, East African Asians and, especially, Pakistanis and Bangladeshis were less likely to own consumer durables than even their income levels would suggest, while the Chinese were rather more likely to.

Evandrou (2000) examined deprivation as well as income among older people specifically. She found substantial levels of deprivation among the older population as a whole, with one in five being deprived on three or more measures. There was some variation by ethnic group, however, with Indian and White elders experiencing the lowest levels of multiple deprivation (around the average) but the rate rose to around a half for Pakistanis and Bangladeshis, with Black Caribbeans (around two fifths) and Irish elders (around a quarter) in between. Pakistanis and Bangladeshis were also the most likely to suffer very high levels of deprivation.

Moore (2000) used the Sample of Anonymised Records from the 1991 Census to examine material deprivation in England based on an index constructed from measures of car ownership, overcrowding and the number of adults in employment, focusing on children of different ethnicities. He also split England into 'poor' and 'not-poor' local authorities. He found that 27% of Bangladeshi children fell into the most deprived group compared to 2% overall, and that this extreme disadvantage clearly differentiated them from Pakistani children, where only 9% were in the most deprived group. In fact, Black African children were the second most deprived group. Black Caribbean and Black Other children had higher than average levels of deprivation, while Indians were close to the average, but showed some overrepresentation in both the most and the least deprived categories.

Poor housing quality is, as mentioned, a potentially important measure of deprivation and there are a number of studies illustrating the different housing conditions of those from different ethnic groups. Harrison (2003) provides a valuable overview of issues in considering ethnic differences in housing experience. He also points to some major gaps in our knowledge, such as the extent of housing assets, relationships with lenders and the housing situation of and response by local authorities to newer immigrants. Dale et al (1996) constructed an index of housing amenity and found that Bangladeshis were most disadvantaged in relation to it, followed by Black Africans. Ratcliffe (1997) showed that in England in the early 1990s twice as many of those from Asian and Black groups than from White groups were living in houses in the worst state of repair. In Scotland, Pakistanis were found to have the greatest levels of housing deprivation (Netto et al, 2001). High levels of overcrowding among Bangladeshis were also demonstrated in England (Ratcliffe, 1997; see also Kempson, 1999). And Pakistani owner–occupation tended to be in the older terraces of inner cities. Ballard (1996b) and Bowes and Sim (2002) have drawn attention to the poor quality or lack of amenity in housing occupied by Pakistanis. In their study of former and current council housing in

England, Peach and Byron (1994) showed that Black Caribbeans in local authority housing were more likely to be living in flats or maisonettes than in houses; and those living in flats were more likely to be on high floors. And Bangladeshis in local authority accommodation have tended to be allocated in the least desirable properties (Ratcliffe, 1997). The Chinese population, along with the Indian population, appear to hold a relatively strong housing position (Phillips, 1997); but a substantial segment of the Chinese population also live in non-self-contained flatted accommodation (Ratcliffe, 1997). Minority ethnic groups have also been shown to be at greater risk of homelessness (Netto, 2006).

In Newham, a single poor area of high housing demand and great poverty, levels of housing stress[1] might be expected to be fairly similar across the population. In effect the impact of 'neighbourhood' is discounted. It was clear from Platt's (2003a) analysis that levels of housing stress within the borough were clearly related to tenure type, with social housing being associated with the highest levels of housing stress. It was also clear that stress levels across tenures were higher than those in Britain for the same tenure type. Absolute differences in housing stress were extremely large for Bangladeshi households (41% were suffering housing stress) and large for Caribbean, Black African, Pakistani, Other and Mixed households, where the rates were all over 30% compared to the White rate of under 20%.

The ability to build up or replace goods or to maintain or renovate housing is clearly related not only to current income but also to long-term financial history and prospects. I consider issues of poverty duration below, but prospects for the future and willingness to accumulate debt are also relevant to whether deprivation is experienced in the present and how closely it relates to income.

Subjective measures

How people perceive their poverty status is an area that is particularly underdeveloped in relation to ethnic group differences. However, a study of a Newham compared the financial optimism of White groups, Caribbeans and Pakistanis in Britain and Newham, controlling for a range of household and family characteristics (Platt, 2003a). It found that Pakistanis were least optimistic about their future financial situation while Caribbeans were most optimistic, with the White groups in between. This held for men and women, although women were less financially optimistic than men.

Another form of subjective measure of financial situation is money worries. Analysis of the Fourth National Survey of Ethnic Minorities revealed that Caribbeans experienced more debt and anxiety than the other minority groups and more than their income levels implied (Berthoud, 1997). It is possible that it is uncertainty rather than actual current income that is affecting Caribbeans in relation to money worries. The role of fluctuations in income in creating income insecurity deserves further attention more generally (Platt, 2006e). Fluctuations in income may cause more anxiety than continuous, but reliable low income.

This could be supported by the evidence that pensioners are less likely to have durables, but also less likely to report arrears or financial anxiety.

Extra costs

Differences in extra costs for those of different ethnic groups can result from differences in the costs of available goods and services; differences in the costs of goods and services to meet particular socially determined standards of living; and also the extra costs of disability and childcare provision, which may be more prevalent among particular ethnic groups. The experience of discrimination, isolation or exclusion may also form a kind of additional cost in the sense of heightened penalty for an equal income level, among minority ethnic groups in poverty (Netto et al, 2001). Again the research base in this area is not extensive. However, there are some suggestions of areas that might indicate that particular ethnicities may experience extra costs.

Based on a small study of Bangladeshi (Muslim) families in Tower Hamlets, Oldfield et al (2001) adjusted the budget standards calculation of minimum costs of a non-poor existence (Parker, 1998) to take account of culturally specific aspects of lifestyle and expenditure. They found that for Bangladeshis living in Tower Hamlets, it took more money to meet a Low Cost but Acceptable standard of living. Extra costs that required a higher budget for Bangladeshi families with two children, compared to White families with two children living in the East End (Parker, 2001), included higher food costs, some extra clothing costs and Arabic lessons for children.

Many of the Bangladeshi women in Phillipson et al's (2003) study also identified children's religious education as a substantial additional expense, which they funded through 'going without' themselves. They also stated that they prioritised the needs of their children above their own immediate needs, consistent with Middleton and Ashworth's (1995) study on mothers more generally. Cohen et al (1992) illustrated the difficulties of participating in traditional practices for those existing on Income Support. For example, the authors presented findings that children were excluded from important social practices such as religious festivals through the unavailability of funds for new clothing.

In her study of poverty among the 'invisible' community of gypsies in Britain, Fitzpatrick (2005) argued that perceptions of what constitutes poverty may be of particular relevance to this group, and highlighted the issue of space. This draws attention to complexities around using standard measures of disadvantage across heterogeneous groups, particularly those who have only limited voice. (See also the discussion of understandings of homelessness in Netto et al, 2004.)

Whether all the income is at the disposal of the household will also make a big difference as to whether a given income level translates into poverty or not. One way in which household income can be reduced is by the transfer of monies to family members outside the household. There is little direct evidence on inter-household income transfers or the transmission of remittances for Britain. What there is suggests that sending money outside the household is most common for Caribbeans (Berthoud, 1997). Phillipson et al (2003) found some evidence of the continual sending of remittances among Bangladeshi families in London, but the scale of it is hard to determine. In the Fourth National Survey of Ethnic Minorities, a third of Caribbeans were found to send money to other family members – in the majority of cases, as for all minority groups, this was going abroad – and they were also the group most likely to do so regularly (Berthoud, 1997). This is despite the fact that, as Berthoud points out, this is the group with the longest average duration in Britain and the most likely to have been born in Britain. It would normally be expected that remittances decrease with time since migration as well as with level of 'integration' in the country, as is found in studies of Germany (Merkle and Zimmermann, 1992; Holst and Schrooten, 2006). However, Boneham (2000), in her study of older people from minority groups in Liverpool, found that, despite the fact that her respondents were past retirement age, over a quarter of them sent money or gifts overseas. Berthoud (1997) found that those with very low incomes were less likely to send remittances, but beyond that there was little association between income level and sending remittances. (A lack of association between income and the sending of remittances was also found for Germany – Holst and Schrooten, 2006.)

The implications of this latter finding are twofold: first, that remittances might be an expected or desired use of income, which those who are on very low incomes are unable to afford. There may be an argument therefore for considering whether inability to transfer money is a source of concern and anxiety for some households. It could potentially form a measure of deprivation on similar lines to those relating to social participation. Second, even those with relatively low incomes – even if not the poorest – may be spending money on those outside their households to the potential detriment of co-resident family members.

On the other hand, managed debt can provide a means to tide people over difficult patches. In one study, Bangladeshi women drew on brothers, brothers-in-law, but especially children to help them out with special expenses or to ease more general financial difficulties (Phillipson et al, 2003). Nevertheless, the authors found that only one in five of these women felt they had 'access to cash in an emergency'. Differences in attitudes to debt may mean that sources such as the Social Fund are not necessarily used by some groups (Sadiq-Sangster, 1992).

Severity and duration

As noted above, the extent to which income poverty translates into deprivation and lack of 'necessities' is primarily connected to its severity and/or its duration. From the evidence on deprivation, we might infer that there is greater severity and duration of low income among some of the most deprived groups; however, there is only a limited amount of direct evidence on these two issues. Analysis of the Family Resources Survey for 1994/95 and 1995/96 and the Fourth National Survey of Ethnic Minorities (1993) revealed the extreme position of Pakistanis and Bangladeshis in terms of income levels (Berthoud, 1998b; Berthoud and Beishon, 1997). As well as highlighting differences in the rates of poverty, this also drew attention to the amounts by which incomes differed and the size of the shortfalls for the Pakistanis and Bangladeshis in relation to a minimum needs standard. In a study of Newham, median poverty gaps were calculated (that is, the midpoint for each group of the distance below the poverty line of those in poverty) to give some grasp of severity of poverty among the poor (Platt, 2003a). Median poverty gaps were largest for the Other White group, and substantially higher than the average for Bangladeshis, Black Africans and Indians. Platt's (2003b) study combined information on severity and duration using Housing Benefit data for Birmingham from the late 1990s. It showed the cumulative impact of a shortfall in income relative to needs. This was shown to impact most on Bangladeshis, and be less significant for Caribbeans.

There is little direct evidence on poverty durations and ethnicity. For overall patterns the Department for Work and Pensions produces an annual analysis of the British Household Panel Survey; however, this is not able to differentiate by ethnic group. The limited number of studies that have information on poverty durations by ethnic group include a short panel study of Newham over three years, 2001-04, which has sufficient numbers from certain minority ethnic groups to allow some analysis of poverty persistence (Buck, 2004; Jäckle and Buck, 2005); and a study of movements into and out of means-tested benefit receipt in Birmingham in the late 1990s (Platt, 2003b, 2006a).

Analysis of poverty persistence in the Newham data started from a base of very high poverty rates across the population and higher risks of poverty for selected characteristics than in Britain as a whole (Platt, 2003a). Overall, movements into and out of poverty were higher in Newham than for the overall population, consistent with a population where many are near to the poverty line and so small fluctuations take them in or out (Buck, 2004; Jäckle and Buck, 2005), although some movement is likely to be caused by instability in measurement. Nevertheless, persistence in poverty between the first two waves of the panel was also greater in Newham than in Britain. Those ethnic groups that had experienced the most poverty in the first wave of the panel – Pakistani, Bangladeshi and Black African groups – also had the highest rates of persistence in poverty across the three waves of the panel. Persistence in poverty was also found to be associated with higher levels of material deprivation, across the sample.

Platt's (2003b) investigation of poverty persistence among children, using means-tested benefits as a proxy for poverty, showed that for children who were ever on means-tested benefits, poverty persistence was greatest among children in White families. Children from Bangladeshi and Pakistani families who were ever poor were more likely to experience a pattern of moves into and out of benefit.

Given the higher prevalence of poverty among these groups in the first place, this implied that the majority of Bangladeshi children were living on the margins of poverty. Despite the high rates of lone parenthood among Caribbean parents they still had lower poverty persistence than other groups. These differences were partly, but only partly, a consequence of differences in other characteristics across groups that were related to durations of poverty.

Using the same data, Platt (2006e) modelled durations on means-tested benefits and explored characteristics associated with both exit and re-entry. Multivariate analysis showed that, controlling for relevant characteristics, Bangladeshis had lower chances of leaving benefit and higher chances of re-entry than their White peers. On the other hand, Caribbeans had rates of benefit exit that were no different from their White UK peers and lower rates of benefit re-entry. Indians and Pakistanis did not differ significantly from their White UK counterparts in their chances of exiting benefit, but they were more likely to re-enter. Thus, income instability and fluctuations in income sources would appear to be a particular issue for some groups. In addition, the ability to move a clear distance out of poverty without risking re-entry would appear to be harder for some groups than others. Income instability may have impacts on welfare in addition to the impact of poverty itself, perhaps particularly for families with children (Platt, 2006e). The impact of income insecurity merits greater attention.

In sum, then, this chapter has described general patterns of poverty and ethnicity and their variation, particularly in relation to income poverty. And the story told is largely consistent across studies and measures. However, there are a number of areas in which our knowledge is scanty.

What has not been explored in relation to ethnicity and poverty?

- We lack recent detailed analysis of household incomes and poverty rates by ethnic group for the UK and, as far as it would be feasible, for the countries of the UK. The same is true for household incomes of 'new immigrants' and of Gypsy and Traveller groups.
- We lack information on durations of poverty and the dynamics of poverty among minority ethnic groups, with the exception of the study of benefit dynamics discussed above (Platt, 2003b, 2006e). The need for information on moves into and out of poverty was also stressed by Netto et al (2001). The issue of income insecurity deserves greater attention generally.
- There is only a small amount of evidence on inter-household transfers and remittances in particular. Greater understanding of their impact on household income and their meaning for the households concerned would be valuable.
- There is little information on subjective experiences of poverty and how these do or do not vary across groups. Whether understandings of poverty vary with ethnicity and what the reference is for perceptions of financial well-being remains a largely open question.

Note

[1] Here, housing stress is defined as experiencing two or more of the following housing problems: shortage of space, not enough light, lack of adequate heating, condensation, having a leaky roof, damp floors and walls, and rot in windows and floors.

Part Three
Explaining ethnic differences in poverty

In this Part we turn to possible levels of explanation for the reasons why certain ethnic groups have higher rates of poverty than others. One form of explanation is to contrast general characteristics that increase poverty risks that are overrepresented among some ethnic groups (for example, lone-parent families), with characteristics that can be considered specific to particular groups and that increase their rates of poverty (for example, norms of labour market non-participation among married women – Platt, 2002). It is clearly, however, not meaningful to separate these out. Issues of family form or labour market participation of women do not exist in a vacuum but relate to perceived opportunities and structures. The costs involved in changing as well as maintaining particular family patterns or forms of community will also be influenced by context. Both forms of explanation can, then, be looked at in relation to structures and individual actions/behaviours.

The following chapters return to Figure 1.1 in Chapter One to organise the discussion of causes and factors contributing to or associated with poverty, and in relation to ethnicity. Thus, there follows a chapter related to factors associated with labour market involvement and earnings. Subsequent chapters cover household structure and family form, and issues of eligibility and take-up in relation to benefit receipt. The accrual of assets, savings and pension entitlements is largely linked to income, and thus to earnings and employment histories across the lifecourse, and to family expenditure (Nesbitt and Neary, 2001) and caring constraints, and so will not merit a separate discussion outside the chapters on employment, family structure and social security.

The organisation of the chapters, by considering aspects in different sections, suggests that causes can be separated out in relation to their effects on poverty. However, that is clearly not strictly the case, even if distinct bodies of literature exist around health, employment, education, discrimination and so on. Works on minority ethnic groups– or minority ethnic disadvantage – will nevertheless tend to divide areas in a similar fashion (see, for example, Mason, 2003b; Modood et al, 1997); although Heath and Yu (2005), when attempting to explain minority ethnic disadvantage, used a rather broader approach, looking at human capital, discrimination and assimilation and evaluating arguments in all three areas in relation to the disparities they found. In this book, while adopting the practical, if somewhat artificial, arrangement of distinguishing some 'topics', I draw on Heath and Yu's attempt not simply to summarise but also to evaluate arguments in relation to a particular focus – in their case minority ethnic disadvantage, in this case differences in poverty for different ethnic groups. In the process, I acknowledge that when looking at the 'causes of poverty' these all shape each other just as they shape the meaning and experience of ethnicity – and are affected by it (Mason, 2003c).

It remains likely, however, that greater consideration could still usefully be paid to how we think across the sections of the following account. One particular way in which 'reading across' is very important is in relation to issues of gender and generation. Differences between men and women, particularly in relation to labour market experiences, may be more fundamental than differences between ethnic groups (Iganski and Payne, 1996; Mason, 2003c). However, the way in which gender patterns experiences of poverty and sources of poverty may also vary across groups. Thus, the chances of low earnings and the link between low earnings and living in a low-income household may not be meaningful if gender is excluded from consideration. For example, much research on employment – and pay in particular – has tended to focus on male earnings. Similarly, issues related to life stage, to children, and to older people in particular, may dominate experience and risks of poverty. In what follows, I attempt to be sensitive as to how espoused causes of poverty vary/might vary with gender and gendered distributions, as well as with age/cohort and between 'new migrants' and settled ethnic groups. Gender also forms a dominant element of the discussion in Chapter Six. However, the review is, again, dependent on the nature of the discussion in the sources and what can be garnered from them.

FIVE

Income from employment

This chapter covers factors associated with both the chances of being in employment and thus in receipt of earnings that can contribute to household income, and what can help to explain the particular rewards from that employment in terms of earnings. As Chapter Four illustrated, there are big absolute differences between ethnic groups in both employment and unemployment rates and in terms of pay. Heath (2001) has argued that unemployment is the crucial issue; and it has also been claimed that employment differentials are much more important to differences in ethnic group outcomes than pay once in employment (Clark and Drinkwater, 2007); but, as was seen from the tables in Chapter Four, differences in pay between groups are also stark.

In attempting to understand differences in employment chances and rates of pay, a number of studies have focused predominantly on individual characteristics, and have concentrated on those 'deficits' in terms of equal competition in the labour market that might be associated with immigrant status per se. Thus, this body of literature focuses on those with immigrant backgrounds and examines factors such as:

- levels of education/qualifications and whether those qualifications (or years of schooling) were obtained in the UK or abroad;
- lack of fluency in English language;
- lack of familiarity with job-search institutions;
- more limited networks;
- lack of translation of human capital across national boundaries or failure of employers to recognise qualifications gained abroad.

In this literature, the primary focus is on the immigrants' background and 'ethnicity' may be used to distinguish within these migrants on the basis either of information on country of birth or of ethnic identification. This evidence is examined in the first section of this chapter. However, such disadvantage would be expected to disappear over time, as immigrants become increasingly familiar with host institutions, increase their networks, become more fluent in English, acquire locally recognised qualifications and so forth. The literature considered provides some evidence that disadvantage does diminish with time since migration, and that employment chances improve for the British born (Clark and Drinkwater, 2007). Nevertheless, there is also substantial evidence of disadvantage accruing or continuing for the 'second generation'.

The second section goes on to consider the outcomes for the 'second generation', where disadvantages associated specifically with the fact or process of immigration are no longer relevant. It considers the extent to which outcomes for ethnic groups are comparable when a more limited range of relevant characteristics, notably education, are held constant. Differences in educational attainment are first discussed and then the disparities in outcome that remain for particular ethnic groups, when, once again, like with like is compared.

In this analysis of ethnicity and ethnic penalties, while the focus is on research on the British-born generation(s) who have experienced a comparable educational and institutional context, it is not just the stage of life but the analytical approach that distinguishes analysis of immigration from analysis of ethnicity, as discussed in Chapter Two. Overall, the evidence does not suggest a substantial diminution in ethnic penalties compared to the first generation. This, although of concern, is not so surprising from a perspective that takes the stratified nature of society across a number of levels as a core assumption, rather than perceiving individuals as somehow free-floating from structural processes of inclusion and exclusion. On this basis disadvantage can be cumulative over time and can become embedded in particular contexts.

Two frameworks have been put forward for explaining remaining differences between ethnic groups (or immigrants) in outcomes that can be shown even after relevant characteristics have been accounted for:

- First, it is argued that there are characteristics that are relevant to the attainment of employment or to particular levels of pay that it has not been possible to take account of in the analytical model (for example, Hatton and Tani, 2005).
- Second, that all the unexplained gap between employment chances on the basis of measured characteristics and actual employment chances for particular minority ethnic group members can be accounted for by 'discrimination' (for example, Denny et al, 1997).

In actuality, the full story is that it is probably some combination of the two. Heath and McMahon (1997) coined the term 'ethnic penalty' to describing this gap in outcomes after controlling for characteristics. This term was used to allow both the fact that 'ethnic effects' that remained when like was compared with like could not simply be 'read off' as a measure of discrimination, but it also acknowledges that discrimination plays a part in it. Thus, while not dismissing attempts to explain the penalty through more accurate comparisons and specification of relevant factors, it also highlighted that there was a prima facie case for discrimination.

Introducing discrimination into the discussion can begin to show how discrimination and racism can affect outcomes and also how they can shape other characteristics that might be seen as 'individual characteristics'.

Consideration of such structural factors can also reveal how looking for understanding of differences purely in individual characteristics may miss much of the point. The investigations are based on the premise of comparing like with like, with the assumption that if absolute differences in employment outcomes can be explained by reference to educational attainment or long-term illness or location then they cease to represent a problem of inequality. However, groups may be so different in their characteristics that such a comparison is not especially meaningful. Moreover, those very characteristics will be shaped, at least in part, by exposure to particular opportunities and constraints. 'Preferences', as discussed in the Introduction (p 12), are only meaningful in the extent to which they can realistically be exercised.

The second section of the chapter therefore moves on to a consideration of the evidence on racism, discrimination and harassment as factors that reflect an interplay between the individual and social structures and constraints. The final section considers questions of employment opportunity and location.

The role of individual characteristics in employment outcomes

The situation of immigrants

If there are differences in employment, is that simply because those with greater skills, qualifications and experience are more likely to be in work than those without? We know that there are substantial differences in levels of educational achievement by ethnicity — as well as time spent in education (Drew et al, 1997), and that these patterns vary by sex. Figure 5.1 illustrates rates of employment by levels of qualification at 2004, broken down by ethnic group (but excluding Bangladeshis because of small sample sizes). It would suggest that education makes a big difference to minority ethnic groups' outcomes, but also that the chances of employment vary substantially by ethnic group for given levels of education. But individuals in these groups will also vary on a range of other characteristics, including whether or not they were born in Britain. So this section first turns to the literature that focuses on immigrant outcomes and that aims to understand them in a framework of individual characteristics.

Research on employment outcomes among immigrants, predominantly based on analysis of the Labour Force Survey, gives clear evidence of both the importance of education in influencing employment prospects and the penalties associated with certain immigrant backgrounds. In a study of Labour Force Survey data from 1993/94, education and other characteristics were important influences on employment chances. But, while White migrants faced a temporary penalty over and above this, minority ethnic immigrants faced an enduring one — that is, length of time in the UK did not eliminate it (Wheatley Price, 2001a, 2001b). Dustmann and Fabbri (2005a) used 20 years of the Labour Force Survey for Britain up to 2004 to reveal the particular disadvantage of immigrant women in the labour market and the disadvantage of those of Pakistani and Bangladeshi

Figure 5.1: Employment rates by highest qualification and ethnic group, 2004

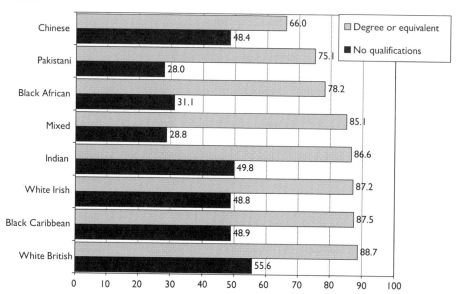

Source: Annual Population Survey, Office for National Statistics

ethnicity in terms of participation and pay, once education was taken account of. Dustmann and Theodoropoulos (2006), also using the Labour Force Survey, looked at penalties in relation to educational achievement for immigrant men and women, and found a disparity between their earnings and employment rates and their levels of qualifications and years of schooling.

Shields and Wheatley Price (1998) used the Labour Force Survey for 1992-94 to examine pay among immigrant men. Their account is of interest for its attempt to take account of the double selection issue in pay data in the Labour Force Survey, that is, that only the pay of those in work is observed and among those in work only the pay of those who respond to the question on pay. Their conclusions emphasise the differences in pay between immigrant and British born of the same ethnic group, after controlling for education and experience and various other relevant characteristics. Consistent with evidence on the assimilation of pay over time (Clark and Lindley, 2004), they show a reduction in ethnic penalties in pay in the second generation, even if not necessarily in employment rates. They also stress the diversity in pay and returns to education and experience among White immigrants.

On the other hand, Denny et al (1997) used a pooled sample of the General Household Survey from 1974 to 1993 to consider differences between immigrant and native earnings across the whole of the wage distribution. Using a distinction within the survey questionnaire between 'White' and 'non-White' that is unrelated to country of birth they found that after taking account of age, education and various other factors 'White' immigrants faced only a slight earnings penalty by comparison with native White people, while 'non-White' immigrants faced a substantial earnings penalty. They concluded, not only that individual characteristics could not explain wage gaps, but also, importantly given the assumptions of much of the literature, that immigrant status may not be the critical determining factor in wage discrimination.

One reason why controlling for educational qualifications may not be an entirely clear indication of expected employment success is for reasons of comparability in qualifications obtained outside the UK. Those ethnic groups composed of a substantial proportion of immigrants will also contain a large number of those with qualifications obtained abroad. It is clear that qualifications obtained abroad are less salient in the labour market than those obtained in Britain (Cheng and Heath, 1993; Bell, 1997; Shields and Wheatley Price, 1998; Blackaby et al, 2002). Whether this evidence is interpreted as employer discrimination, a genuine mismatch between what overseas qualifications represent in relation to skills in the British labour market, or something between the two, in terms of employers' difficulty of interpreting them accurately, is hard to determine.

An issue related to the question of the valuing of British qualifications over foreign ones is the valuing of experience obtained in the UK over experience obtained prior to migration. Human capital is usually considered as a combination of years spent working plus qualifications. But it is clear that it matters where work took place. Thus, the employment penalty for immigrants reduces with time spent in the UK (Bell, 1997; Frijters et al, 2005). Again the extent to which this is to do with the nature of the experience, a failure to recognise it or difficulty in 'translating' it to the UK context is debated. In one study, among those seeking employment there was a feeling that Jobcentre Plus did not adequately support those with overseas experience and qualifications in making good use of them in the UK context (Hudson et al, 2006).

Attention has also been paid to English language fluency as a further element of human capital. Lack of proficiency in spoken English may impede immigrants' ability to engage in the same sorts of jobs or the same levels (Gazioglu, 1996). Dustmann and Fabbri (2003) showed that language fluency was related to employment probabilities for migrants in England and Wales and that lack of fluency resulted in reduced pay. Shields and Wheatley Price (2002) also found a positive association between English language fluency among immigrants and pay. (See also O'Leary et al, 2001; Shields and Wheatley Price, 2001; Lindley, 2002a.) Leslie and Lindley (2001) also used the Fourth National Survey of Ethnic Minorities to examine the role of fluency in labour market outcomes, and found that it explained some although not all 'non-White' disadvantage. For men, lack of fluency was linked to higher unemployment risks and lower pay; for women to greater rates of economic inactivity. An in-depth, qualitative study of barriers to employment among Pakistanis and Bangladeshis found that lack of English language fluency was related to other barriers to employment (Tackey et al, 2006).

Dustmann (1999) found that the length of stay in the host country was relevant to investment in language acquisition (see also Dustmann and van Soest, 2004).

Research on immigrants' labour market position does indeed seem to show that human capital only explains a small part of the differences between immigrant groups and White British born; although this is not always to the detriment of the immigrant group. Dustmann and Fabbri (2005b) investigated the employment and earnings of women relative to the 'economic potential' of their husbands. They found that White immigrant women had an earnings advantage and that the husbands of White immigrant wives appeared to do better in the labour market than their measured characteristics might predict. This example also highlights the fact that it may be inappropriate to consider the outcomes for individuals independently of their partnership or family context. Just as poverty is measured at the level of the household, and so information on individual outcomes can only be obliquely related to poverty, so it may well be important to consider jointly the employment experiences and labour market strategies of husbands and wives, especially in the particular circumstances following migration (Baker and Benjamin, 1997). (See also the discussion in Platt, 2006d.)

Consistent with findings on the limited impact of human capital among migrants is research on the role of social class background. Heath and McMahon (2005) used pooled data from the General Household Survey for 1985-1992 and covering Britain to examine social class outcomes (access to the 'Salariat' or the professional/managerial social class) taking account of social class background. They found that among first-generation men, Irish men had no differences in chances of access to the higher social class (or 'salariat') compared to White British men once class background was taken into account whereas the chances for Indian, Caribbean and Pakistani men were lower. For women, first-generation Irish and Black Caribbean women had higher chances of access to higher social class outcomes, controlling for background and Indian and Pakistani women had lower chances than White British women.

The results for women are worth noting: the positive outcomes for Irish and Black Caribbean migrants are possibly explained by the targeted migration to take up nursing posts in the expanding National Health Service (NHS). Overall, these results raise the possibility that language is playing a role in the poorer outcomes in the 'first generation' for Pakistani and Indian men and women, even though that would not really explain the outcomes for first-generation Caribbean men.[1]

It is possible that immigrants will have less knowledge or fewer options in relation to searching for jobs, with consequent impact on their unemployment rates. They may have limited knowledge of local labour market institutions or smaller social networks, or be looking in particular sectors of the labour market. Battu et al (2004) argued that personal networks are a popular method of job search for men and women, but that Pakistani and Bangladeshi groups and those born outside the UK were disadvantaged in the labour market as a result of relying on personal networks for job search. By contrast, Frijters et al (2005), using the same data, found some differences in job-search behaviour across their four broad groups of immigrants (South Asian immigrants, Black immigrants, White immigrants, Other immigrants) compared to White non-migrants. However, they found that for all groups, personal contacts were the most effective way of leaving unemployment and that choice of methods of searching for jobs could not explain the immigrant groups' penalty in the longer time it took to leave unemployment. Heath and Yu (2005) considered whether networks for job access had potential for accounting for the outcomes for some groups better than for others. Their evidence does not point to job-search activity or approach as playing an important role in differential employment outcomes. Research exploring specifically the degree of satisfaction with the support offered by Jobcentre Plus to minority ethnic claimants seeking work, showed that job centres were regarded as an important source of information on vacancies but that overall satisfaction with the service provided tended to be lower for minority ethnic groups than for the White majority (Johnson and Fidler, 2006). Claimants from Black groups seemed to have the highest levels of dissatisfaction. This may suggest, additionally, that making use of formal routes for employment is less satisfactory for those from some minority ethnic groups.

Employment disadvantage in the second generation

For the immigrant generation, then, it would appear that 'human capital' has a role to play in absolute differences in employment and pay but that ethnic penalties remain and the anticipated reduction in disadvantage over time is not clearly evident. The approach also tends to assume that the characteristics employed to investigate the employment penalty (such as foreign qualifications and experience) are legitimate causes of poorer employment outcomes.

But what about the second generation? For those who have grown up in Britain, issues of language, qualifications obtained abroad, limited networks and particular job-search activities should not apply, or at least, for the latter two, not to the same extent, given the opportunities for engaging through schooling with different networks and models. Thus, the only factors that *should* determine differences in employment experiences should be where people started in terms of social class backgrounds and the levels of qualifications they have achieved, as well as their age, representing the stage they are at in their work history, and possibly their health status.

Heath and McMahon's (2005) study of the role of social class background, discussed above, found that for the second generation, Irish and Indian men had superior chances of ending up in higher social class outcomes, compared to White British of the same cohort and controlling for class background, but Caribbeans had worse chances. For second-generation women, however, ethnicity no longer played a significant role in outcomes for women once class background was controlled. This can be compared to a similar result found in a comparable analysis of the Longitudinal Study for England and Wales (Platt, 2005b). These findings suggest that class background may have less salience for some ethnic groups than others – but the fact that this would appear to operate differently for men and women is interesting. Of course, looking simply at social class background does not take account of how that class background is – or is not – mediated through education, and the extent to which these results are explicable on the basis of different levels of qualifications according to ethnicity and sex.

Education can be measured in two ways: the stock of qualifications in the population generally and the attainment of qualifications by those who have just (or fairly recently) finished compulsory education. The former can be informative in indicating why employment rates and the rewards of work might vary between groups in relation to differences in educational achievement. The latter measure is potentially informative about the future, and avoids considerations of the role of immigration and the meaning or value of qualifications from abroad, discussed above. It is the stock that will be determining the current employment outcomes of minority ethnic groups, as those just finishing compulsory education will not yet be in the labour market in substantial numbers.

In relation to the stock of qualifications in the population as a whole, Table 5.1 shows the highest qualification held among the population of Britain, by ethnic group and sex. The very high levels of degrees among the Chinese, the White Irish and Indian and Black African men stand out. The Irish, however, seem to have both a very highly educated but also a less well-educated component. The low levels of qualifications among Pakistani and Bangladeshi women and to a lesser extent men and among Black Caribbean men are also noteworthy. The relatively poor performance of White British women, at least compared to men, is also clear. The reasons for these differences are partly to do with the composition of groups, with large numbers of students among Black Africans and a substantial proportion of Bangladeshi and Pakistani women immigrating as adults with few qualifications. On the other hand, the majority of the Black Caribbean men will have been brought up in Britain, and therefore their lower rates of success are a particular cause for concern. White women will tend to have an older distribution than minority ethnic group women, with some of them having left school up to 45 years previously, when education was generally considered a much lower priority for girls than for boys. (For further discussion of the factors influencing the current educational distribution, see Modood, 1997c; Drew, 1995.) The educational distributions of the current working age can, therefore, be expected to change as new cohorts pass through the school system (as we see below).

So how, or to what extent, do differences in educational achievement translate into the differences in employment experience illustrated in Chapter Four? Heath and McMahon (1997) used the 1991 Census (for England, Wales and Scotland) to examine the role of educational attainment in social class outcomes for the second generation. They found it played an important role, but that an 'ethnic penalty' still remained for Black Caribbean, Black African, Indian and Pakistani

Table 5.1: Highest qualification by ethnic group and sex, among men and women of working age, 2004

	Degree or equivalent	Higher education qualification	GCE A level or equivalent	GCSE grades A* to C or equivalent	Other qualification	No qualification
Males						
White British	18	8	30	19	10	14
White Irish	23	6	24	12	17	18
Mixed	22	6	24	20	13	15
Indian	30	6	17	11	22	15
Pakistani	15	4	15	16	22	29
Bangladeshi	11	2	10	12	25	40
Black Caribbean	11	6	26	24	15	18
Black African	24	9	18	14	25	12
Chinese	33	4	13	10	21	19
Females						
White British	16	10	19	29	10	16
White Irish	25	13	15	15	16	16
Mixed	20	7	22	27	13	11
Indian	21	6	16	16	24	18
Pakistani	10	4	14	20	18	35
Bangladeshi	5	2	12	17	15	49
Black Caribbean	15	13	16	33	14	10
Black African	17	9	15	15	26	18
Chinese	29	6	10	8	26	21

Source: Annual Population Survey, Office for National Statistics

men relative to British-born White men (Bangladeshi, Chinese and Other Asian men were excluded from the sample due to small sample sizes). They found a similar story for the ethnic penalties experienced by second-generation women from the different ethnic groups, although minority ethnic group women were even more disadvantaged in relation to avoiding unemployment. They concluded that 'being born in Britain is not associated with any improvement in competitive chances' (Health and McMahon, p 108) – relative to the first generation's social class disadvantage. (See also Heath and Cheung, 2006.)

Clark and Drinkwater (2007) compared employment probabilities at 1991 to those at 2001 for men and women from different ethnic groups for England and Wales. They also looked at the effects of religion on outcomes at 2001. While they found that education played a strong role in explaining employment chances, a big gap between employment probabilities of certain minority ethnic groups and the White majority remained. Comparison of women's outcomes a decade apart using pooled Labour Force Survey data also showed both the increasing relevance of educational qualifications to women's outcomes but also the persistence of the ethnic penalty over time (Lindley et al, 2006). Indeed, this study showed that the extent of differences in employment rates that could be attributed to observed differences between White majority and minority ethnic groups actually decreased over time, leaving a larger role for an 'ethnic penalty'. So, while the fastest increases in educational qualifications have been among Pakistani and Bangladeshi women, and while the differences in employment rates between highly qualified and unqualified are starkest for these groups, employment outcomes do not mirror very closely patterns of educational success and failure. Greater investment in education would appear to bring diminishing returns for some groups. The finding of a strong role for education in employment outcomes, but a persistent ethnic penalty, was also found in a number of other studies, and that it was clearly evident for the UK-born as well as for non-UK minority ethnic groups, specifically for those from Black, Indian and Pakistani groups (Blackaby et al, 1997, 1999, 2002, 2005).

The subject of 'over-education' among minority ethnic group members in work has received extensive discussion and analysis (Battu and Sloane, 2003). Evidence of 'over-qualification' from the Fourth National Survey of Ethnic Minorities suggested that minority ethnic groups were not getting appropriate returns to qualifications, and that this was true across the minority ethnic groups (Battu and Sloane, 2004). Moreover, being UK born and being fluent in English increased – rather than decreased – the mismatch between qualifications and jobs for minority ethnic groups.

From analysis of pay differentials, the vast majority of the difference in pay between White groups and the Indian group and between White and Black groups was attributable to different returns on their characteristics rather than different characteristics (Blackaby et al, 2002). That is, it was not the fact that they were different from the majority that resulted in pay differences but that they got lower rewards for given levels of qualifications and so on. The proportion explained by characteristics was rather greater for the Pakistani group, but still left an unexplained deficit, which the authors attributed to discrimination. Carmichael and Woods (2000) also found penalties for minority ethnic groups in the occupational status of the jobs taken, after controlling for education and other relevant characteristics. They attributed these penalties to discrimination in the labour market operating at the level of occupational distributions. Discrimination – or the failure of equal opportunities policies – is also the conclusion arrived at in a study of differentials in training opportunities (Shields and Wheatley Price, 1999). Differences in characteristics failed to account for the majority of the differences in training between minority and majority ethnic groups, and this was the case for men and even more so for women.

Frijters et al (2005) used overlapping panels from the Labour Force Survey starting between Spring 1997 and Winter 2000 to examine men's unemployment durations. They found that chances of leaving unemployment were lower for British-born minority ethnic groups (all grouped together), despite the fact that their higher qualifications and younger age profile should have made their chances better. They concluded that the part played by employer discrimination in these slower exits from unemployment could not be discounted.

Given that unemployment rates tend to be higher in youth, especially among young men, Berthoud (1999) analysed employment penalties among young men. This enabled him to compare British born/raised with those who migrated to Britain after the age of 16 without the confounding factor that immigrants tend to be older than British-born minority ethnic groups. There were substantial variations in qualifications levels among the young men according to their ethnic group (examining five groups: White, Caribbean, Black African, Indian, and Pakistani or Bangladeshi). And qualifications levels made a big difference to both the White and Caribbean groups, so that they were consistently less likely to be unemployed the more highly they were qualified. To a certain extent, then, high unemployment rates among Caribbeans could be attributed to qualification levels. On the other hand, their chances of unemployment were still greater than those for the White group at all qualification levels.

Qualifications also mattered for risks of unemployment for the other ethnic groups – but much less so. And this could not be related to levels of qualifications across the groups since although the African and Indian groups had high levels of qualifications, Pakistanis and Bangladeshis had relatively low levels of qualifications. The 'returns' to education in terms of unemployment risks seem, therefore, to be unequal across groups from this study as well.

Platt (2005a) in research covering England and Wales found that educational achievement did account for patterns of social mobility for White young people with a migrant background and for Indians and Caribbeans. Education was also an important element in the social class outcomes for White young people with no migration background, although social class background continued to play a strong contributory role for this group, as well. For Pakistanis, their social class position was at odds with their qualifications – they were not getting the rewards from education that they might expect and they suffered far worse employment outcomes both in terms of increased risks of unemployment and lower chances of professional or managerial class outcomes when not only education but also social class background were taken into account. Moreover, the apparent parity between Indians and White non-migrants, once education and social class backgrounds were taken into account, disguised extensive within-group variation (Platt, 2005a).

For Caribbeans it took longer for education to have an effect on class outcomes (Platt, 2005c), and Caribbeans also faced increased risks of unemployment, controlling for social class background (Platt, 2005b), and for social class background and educational qualifications (Platt, 2005a). This latter finding is consistent with Heath and Smith's (2003) argument that higher risks of unemployment are a feature of the experience of the 'second generation' even when taking account of class. The finding on the extended period that qualifications 'need' to take effect for Caribbeans fits with the extended period that all 1991 Census minority ethnic groups spend in post-compulsory education (Drew et al, 1997; Bradley and Taylor, 2004); see also Modood (1998).

While there is extensive discussion of the greater motivation in education for children of migrants in the wider literature (Lauglo, 2000; Card, 2005; Zhou and Xiong, 2005), Drew et al (1997) pointed out that constraints, in terms of limited employment opportunities for young people, of minority ethnicity are also likely to be playing a role in extended periods in education. In addition, Berthoud (2000) found that the benefits of staying on in terms of additional qualifications were not commensurate with the additional time spent acquiring them; and economic considerations did not seem to be the only factor at work in a further study (Leslie and Drinkwater, 1999).

The argument about motivations has also been used to suggest that processes of 'segmented assimilation' (Portes et al, 2005; Zhou and Xiong, 2005) may result in lower motivations for particular minority ethnic groups, through adjustment processes to more limited expectations and through having potentially different reference groups for points of comparison. Thus, it has been argued, for example, that Black Caribbeans in Britain have a reference point of the White working class, which limits their aspirations relative to both the White majority and other minority ethnic groups (Heath and Yu, 2005). However, empirical investigation testing motivation finds that there is little support for the theory of 'adaptation' to lower expectations. Thomas (1998) tested whether attitudes could be seen to have an impact on the length of time spent unemployed and on differences in unemployment duration between those of different ethnicity. This study used the UK Survey of Incomes In and Out of Work from the late 1980s[2] to investigate attitudes to work and their relationship with unemployment durations for five groups (White, Black, Indian, Pakistani/Bangladeshi and 'other non-White'). The analysis demonstrated that taking account of attitudes increased the gap between the chances of leaving unemployment for White groups on the one hand (who left faster) and Indians and Pakistanis/Bangladeshis (who escaped unemployment more slowly). This implied that the three South Asian groups held a greater attachment to the labour market and commitment to finding work than their chances of escaping unemployment warranted. (The results for Black groups were not significantly different from those for the White majority, although their attitudes to employment tended to be more positive.) Moreover, as Heath and Yu (2005) have pointed out, the evidence on differences in retention in education, discussed above, suggests high levels of motivation among minority ethnic groups.

One additional factor that is importantly associated with labour market disadvantage is health status. The relationship between ill-health and labour market position is one of both cause and effect. Disabled people have low employment rates and low pay when they are in work, they also tend to have lower qualifications, although these do not on their own explain their employment disadvantage (Berthoud, 2006). Unemployment and low-paid employment can exacerbate or result in chronic ill-health. Moreover, being from a marginalised group and the impact of racism can also have consequences for the health of vulnerable groups.

There is now a substantial amount of evidence illustrating that social class or poverty has deleterious consequences for health. The Black Report (Townsend and Davidson, 1982) mapped the relationship between social class and health; and Bartley and Plewis (1997) used longitudinal data to show the path of causation from lower social class to poorer health rather than the other way round. We also know that there are clear ethnic differentials in health, with, for example, Pakistani and Bangladeshi women and men having very high (age-standardised) rates of 'not good health' and of 'long-term limiting illness' (Nazroo, 1998; Harding and Balarajan, 2000; National Statistics, 2004b). In England and Wales in 2001, Indian women, White Irish men and Black Caribbean and Other Black men and women also had substantially higher rates of long-term limiting illness than the White British, with only the Chinese and Other White groups having lower rates. In Scotland, Black Scottish/Other Black groups had the highest rates of long-term illness in the 25-34 age range, whereas Pakistanis had the highest rates above age 35 (Scottish Executive, 2004). White British, African and Other ethnic groups had lower rates of long-term illness than White Scottish at all ages. There are a number of studies that show how the factor of class in health outcomes can explain many general findings on ethnic differences in health (Harding and Balarajan, 2000; Chandola, 2001; Nazroo, 2003) or has the potential to (Davey Smith et al, 2000).

Nevertheless, for the purposes of this book, which is to understand why some people are more likely to be in poverty than others, it is the impact of ill-health on sources of income and uses of income that may lead to poverty that is of particular relevance. There is, however, little evidence on how use of health-related benefits among those with comparable health conditions varies with ethnicity (although see the discussion relating to take-up of benefits in Chapter Seven).

We now move briefly from a focus on ethnic differences to consider the small body of literature relating to how labour market outcomes are patterned by religious affiliation. Religious affiliation and ethnicity are clearly distinct but nevertheless have a number of points of overlap, as was discussed in Chapter Two. A small number of studies have focused on the relationship between religious affiliation and labour market outcomes. Brown (Brown, M. S., 2000) used the

Fourth National Survey of Ethnic Minorities to consider whether religion provided a better indicator of labour market disadvantage than ethnic group. His results, which focused on just the three South Asian groups – Indians, Pakistanis and Bangladeshis –challenged the notion of a 'Muslim/non-Muslim dichotomy', pointing to the big differences (after controlling for relevant characteristics) between Indian Hindus and Sikhs in labour market outcomes (with the Sikhs much more disadvantaged than the Hindus); and he also showed that Pakistani and Bangladeshi Muslim men had twice the unemployment rate of Indian Muslim men. Indian Muslim men were, on the other hand, the least likely of any ethno-religious category to be economically inactive. There were also differences among women: Indian Muslim women's rates of economic inactivity fell between those of Indian Sikh and Hindu women on the one hand and Pakistani and Bangladeshi Muslim women on the other (see also Peach, 2006). Using the same source, Lindley's (2002b) results are largely consistent with Brown's, although she tackled the question in a slightly different way, to ascertain if religion can 'fill the gap' presented by the ethnic penalty. That is, whether the ethnic penalty and its variation across ethnic groups is in fact a 'religious penalty'. She broke down religious affiliation by ethnicity and looked at labour market outcomes for both men and women. She concluded that there was a clear 'Islamic penalty' in employment outcomes, that was not attributable to other relevant characteristics.

Ahmad et al (2003) argued strongly that religion was very important to understanding the labour market position of South Asian women. Complementing some analysis of the Fourth National Survey of Ethnic Minorities with a more detailed qualitative study, they attempted to show how educational and occupational 'choices' of educated South Asian women should not be seen as 'oppositional' to their religious identity. They therefore simultaneously stressed the importance of taking account of religious affiliation in exploring labour market outcomes for women (and by implication for men as well), but urged caution about 'stock' interpretations of such findings, in relation to cultural accounts of inactivity or attitudes to the labour market, particularly in relation to women. (See also Ansari, 2002.)

The religion question in the 2001 Census has enabled labour market position to be analysed by religious affiliation as well as or instead of ethnic group. A focus on Muslims has shown that they had the highest unemployment rates and lowest economic activity rates of any faith group (Open Society Institute EU Monitoring and Advocacy Program, 2004). However, the distinction within the Muslim group with Indian Muslims faring rather better and Pakistanis and Bangladeshi Muslims faring rather worse was also evident (Bradford and Forsyth, 2006).

Clark and Drinkwater (2007) also exploited the religion question in the 2001 Census to explore the association of religious affiliation with labour market outcomes in England and Wales. Educational qualifications played an important role in explaining labour market disadvantage across ethnic groups, but religion was also found to have an independent effect. Poorer labour market outcomes were found for Sikhs and Hindus, but especially for Muslims compared to other groups and controlling for relevant characteristics. Jewish men had substantially higher employment probabilities than Christian men. The pattern of Jewish advantage and Sikh and Muslim disadvantage in occupational outcomes, after taking account of education and background and ethnic group, was also illustrated in Platt's (2005a) study of social mobility. This study also showed the same pattern of relative Hindu advantage (alongside the Christian subpopulation) and Sikh and Muslim disadvantage within the Indian ethnic group, consistent with M. S. Brown's (2000) findings (although not found in the Clark and Drinkwater study).

Education appears, then, to be a necessary component of positive employment outcomes – but not necessarily sufficient to avoid an ethnic penalty in employment or pay. But, looking to the future, what are the lifecourse and employment prospects indicated by the achievements of the current or recent generations going through school and how have these achievements themselves been shaped by the experience of poverty of their parents, given the strength of cumulative or intergenerational patterns of disadvantage?

Gillborn and Mirza (2000), reviewing the research on educational inequalities across England and Wales, identified the complexity of achievement patterns. Thus, every one of the minority ethnic groups considered (White, Black Caribbean, Black African, Black Other, Indian, Pakistani and Bangladeshi) was the best performing in at least one of the 118 local education authorities considered. But the general picture of education for those passing through the system currently is one of divergent outcomes between the most and the least successful. Chinese pupils' success stands out with 75% of those in England in 2002/03 achieving five or more GCSEs at grades A⋆ to C, compared to an average of 51% across all pupils (DfES, 2005a). Indian and Irish pupils were also successful at this level with Black African, Mixed White and Black Caribbean, Black Caribbean and Black Other pupils doing progressively less well and all achieving under the average. Pakistani and Bangladeshi children also underperformed relative to the average. The lowest levels of attainment were among Gypsy/Roma children, with 23% getting five or more GCSEs at grades A⋆ to C. Forty-two per cent of Irish Traveller children, however, achieved this level of qualification. In addition, many Traveller and Gypsy/Roma children of secondary school age will not be registered and will thus not appear in the data (Bhattacharyya et al, 2003).

Once broken down by sex the pattern becomes more complex. Girls performed better than boys on average and across all groups except for Irish Travellers and (marginally) Gypsy Roma children. The average difference is 11 percentage points, with 46% of boys and 56% of girls achieving five GCSEs at grades A⋆ to C; but this reaches a difference of 15 percentage points for Bangladeshi children (39% of boys and 53% of girls), Black Caribbean children (25% of boys and 40% of girls), Mixed White and Black Caribbean children (32% of boys and 47% of girls) and Mixed White and Black African children (40% of boys and 55% of girls). This means that Bangladeshi and Mixed White and Black African girls are performing better than White British boys, even though the group average is lower than that for White British children. It also means that Black Caribbean boys are approaching being the least successful group, just above the success rate for Gypsy/Roma children.

These large differences in attainment are indicative of both past processes of access and marginalisation and of future outcomes, to the extent that education is linked with employment and (thereby) with poverty. However, research has shown that in terms of poverty transmission these differences are relatively insensitive to socioeconomic status as indicated by receipt of free school meals. While all those receiving free school meals do worse than their ethnic group counterparts not receiving free school meals, the differences were much more important for some groups than others (see also Sammons, 1995; Wilson et al, 2005).

In summary, then, educational achievement goes a long way to explaining differences in employment outcomes between ethnic groups, illustrated in Chapter Four. However, research has also identified persistent differences that cannot be put down to such human capital causes – however well or variously defined – leaving clear 'ethnic penalties' at least for some groups. These are most consistently evident for Bangladeshis and Pakistanis (both men and women) relative to White groups and for immigrants as a whole, although there are substantial differences between immigrant groups. They are also shown for Caribbeans (particularly Caribbean men) and for Indians (although for women more often than men).

Racism, discrimination and harassment

Discrimination in employment has been illegal for decades and legislation exists to penalise racially motivated crimes. Nevertheless, there is little doubt that discrimination continues to operate to limit the life chances of those in a range of marginalised positions. Definitions of discrimination and institutional racism and the legal framework have been extensively rehearsed elsewhere (Goulbourne, 1998; Parekh, 2000; Connolly, 2002; Bhavnani et al, 2005). This section, will not, therefore, cover these issues. Instead, in line with the discussions in the rest of this chapter, I will investigate the ways in which discrimination can affect employment chances and earnings – and thus the household incomes available to different ethnic groups.

In considering the role of discrimination in affecting employment opportunities and rewards we need to consider both the *mechanisms* by which discrimination has an effect and the *measures* by which its effect is ascertained or inferred. Much of the literature that attributes unexplained ethnic group effects in statistical analyses to discrimination is relatively unforthcoming about the mechanisms by which it operates. The implication is that it is direct discrimination by employers, preferring a candidate of one ethnicity over an equally suitable candidate of another ethnicity. However, employer discrimination is only one route, although it may be the most important. And it may not be overt or direct: an investigation at the point of interview found little evidence of direct discrimination in selection but it identified a 'linguistic penalty' in terms of effective communication for first-generation minority ethnic groups (Roberts and Campbell, 2006). Employment discrimination can operate not only at the point of entry into employment but also within employment in relation to access to promotion and related activities, such as training, that may themselves lead to promotion. Within employment, discriminatory attitudes of co-workers can also affect the position of employees from other ethnic groups; and racism by fellow workers may isolate minority ethnic employees, and impact on their experience of the workplace, their job performance and their chances for advancement. Perceptions, or experience, of discrimination by either employers or fellow workers may also affect the behaviour of those discriminated against so that they select what would be otherwise less attractive employment opportunities – or exit from the labour market altogether. Racism on the part of customers, clients or contractors may also affect the employment chances and productivity (and thus rewards) of workers (Holzer and Ihlanfeldt, 1998).

A further way in which discrimination and racism can impact on employment opportunities and rewards is indirectly by shaping situations or choices in other areas that then have an impact on employment. Thus, discrimination in the education system, with its effect on qualifications, and discrimination in housing provision or housing markets, with its effect on where people live and the jobs they have access to, will affect employment experiences and rewards. Moreover, the intimidation caused by racism may influence vulnerable groups' choices about where to live (Harrison, 2003), with consequent effects on employment opportunities. Racism and discrimination may also have an impact on health as well as psychological well-being (Williams and Harding, 2004; Karlsen and Nazroo, 2002), resulting in fewer and poorer employment opportunities. Thus, the effects of discrimination may not be revealed by an analysis of ethnic group differences comparing like with like, as they may be shaping differences in characteristics between groups as well.

Having identified the possible mechanisms, the next issue is what evidence can be used to show that they are operating and who they are affecting. Measurement of discrimination is a complex area and is hard to demonstrate directly. A range of approaches are thus used to identify or imply its existence – some more complex than others. Employer discrimination at the point of job entry can be directly tested through sample applications or telephone inquiries from otherwise equally qualified applicants from different ethnic groups. Such experiments have been used in the past to demonstrate discriminatory practice by employers at the point of selection. However, in the last 15 years there have been few such studies, although the Commission for Racial Equality in Scotland found direct evidence using this approach of discriminatory selection procedures in invitations to interview by employers (Commission for Racial Equality, 1996). According to this study, in the North of England and Scotland, young White people were three times as likely as comparable Asian applicants and five times as likely as African Caribbean applicants to get an interview.

Another indication of levels of employer discrimination can be identified using people's perceptions of personal experience of discrimination. For example, Modood (1997b) used responses on perceived job refusal, with Caribbeans the most likely to identify discriminatory job refusal, at 28%, followed by African Asians, Indians, Chinese and Pakistanis and Bangladeshis. More recently, the Home Office Citizenship Survey canvassed perceptions of discriminatory job refusal. Here it was Black African men (26%) and women (16%) who were most likely to identify job refusal on racial grounds (Heath and Cheung, 2006). See also Connolly and Keenan, 2001. Over 10% of Caribbean and Black Mixed men also perceived they had been denied a job on racial grounds, with smaller, although still substantial, proportions of Indian and Pakistani men and Caribbean women (around 9%) followed by around 7% of Bangladeshi men and Indian and Pakistani women and 6% of Bangladeshi women. Analysis of the 2005 Citizenship Survey, not disaggregated by sex, found that, of those who had been refused a job in the last five years, around 17% of Indians and Pakistanis, over 20% of Caribbeans and nearly 30% of Black Africans felt that the refusal was on racial grounds (Kitchen et al, 2006). The problem here is that people's perceptions may not be accurate; and identifying whether you have been discriminated against at the point of selection (either invitation to interview or following an interview) is very hard to ascertain, given that it is almost impossible to know what the competition is. Nevertheless, such perceptions give some indication of the obstacles those seeking jobs feel face them. A further issue is that there may be less experience or perception of discriminatory job refusal in highly segregated job markets, which might be the most disadvantaging, but where issues of competition do not arise. Thus, increasing perceptions of discrimination in employment could, paradoxically, be a result of a more open labour market with greater opportunities for minority ethnic groups to compete with the majority (Modood, 1997b). In this case, Caribbeans, who are much more dispersed in geographical and occupational terms, have more opportunities to be disfavoured in relation to their White peers. The results could also be influenced by age distributions. Those who are younger are likely to have applied for fewer jobs, especially applications for jobs from existing employment, and will have had fewer opportunities for experiencing discrimination.

Surveys of prejudiced views may act as a general barometer of discriminatory attitudes in the population. According to the British Social Attitudes Survey, at the beginning of the 1990s 36% of the population considered themselves to be racially prejudiced, declining to 25% by the end of the decade before rising again to 32% in the early years of the 21st century (Rothon and Heath, 2003). This rise is consistent with a perceived increase in racial prejudice found in the Home Office Citizenship Survey (Kitchen et al, 2006). Around 30% of those of working age viewed themselves as racially prejudiced in 2003 (Heath and Cheung, 2006). However, their relationship to employer discrimination can only be oblique – only those in a position to appoint or refuse a job can do so. However, these figures may also act as indicators of potential discriminatory attitudes in the working environment and thus link to apparent preferences for, or concentrations of, minority ethnic groups in less prejudiced environments, specifically in public sector rather than private sector occupations (Heath and Cheung, 2006).

Perceptions of discrimination within employment, for example in relation to promotion, are likely to give a much clearer indication of actual discrimination. Some complaints will reach tribunal and tribunal cases and investigations of employers by the Commission for Racial Equality may give some indication of the nature of discriminatory experience that people may face in employment. But few cases reach tribunal; and, again, there is the issue that people may be more likely to take cases where they have greater faith in the effectiveness of the system. In addition, union members may feel better able to take cases against employers and there is some variation in union membership by ethnic group. Brook (2002), in an analysis of the autumn 2001 Labour Force Survey, found that 30% of employees from Black groups compared to 29% of White employees and between 22 and 25% of South Asian, Mixed and Other groups were union members. Tribunals and actions against employers are only likely therefore to be indicative rather than clear evidence of differences in discrimination experience between groups or over time.

A Trades Union Congress hotline in 2000 provided indicative evidence of an underlying volume of discrimination and racism at work (TUC, 2000). Nearly 90 calls a day to the hotline over the course of a week outlined experiences ranging from daily racist abuse, to not being informed about promotion opportunities, to having belongings damaged or experiencing violence, to being refused references. They also highlighted a high degree of complacency at managerial level. The 2005 Citizenship Survey also highlighted the number of people who perceived that a promotion had been denied them on racial grounds. Around 50% of the different minority ethnic groups (from 46% of Indians to 57% of Black Africans) who had been refused a promotion felt it was on racial grounds (Kitchen et al, 2006).

Shields and Wheatley Price (1999) looked at the amount of training received by minority ethnic workers compared to White workers. They found that there were substantial differences, which were greater for women than for men, in employer-funded training, and suggested that such disparities represented a failure of equal opportunities policies. Such differentials in training opportunities have consequences, as the authors point out, for future pay and promotion prospects of minority ethnic group employees. Pudney and Shields (2000) found differences in the speed of promotion in the nursing profession for different ethnic groups, with implications for earnings across the lifecourse. Clark and Drinkwater (2007) found that pay discrepancies were greatest within occupations, suggesting that it is not occupational distributions but relative positions within occupations that result in pay differentials for ethnic groups.

As noted above, employer discrimination is also frequently inferred from the gaps that remain in analyses between outcomes for different ethnic groups after controlling for characteristics. Thus, for example, Carmichael and Woods (2000) argue that differences in employment rates indicate discrimination at the point of selection; and differences in occupational distributions – with a consequent impact on pay – represent discrimination in promotion, training and other factors related to advancement. While, as discussed, there are problems with such assumptions, 'ethnic employment penalties' are likely to provide some indication of ongoing labour market discrimination, particularly if supplemented by perceptions of job applicants, even if direct, employer discrimination may not well account for the whole of the penalty.

It has been argued that White workers may have a 'taste for discrimination'. That is, that majority group workers, for reasons of prestige, status and prejudiced attitudes, may prefer to work alongside other majority group workers and therefore demand a premium in pay for working alongside minority group workers. This theory has been investigated for British workers using matched employer–employee data (Frijters et al, 2004). The study found that, controlling for a range of individual and workplace characteristics, White male employees in workplaces with higher proportions of minority ethnic groups had lower job satisfaction and higher wages than their otherwise similar counterparts in occupations with lower levels of minority ethnic groups. These results are consistent with hypotheses deriving from the theoretical literature in this area that a 'taste for discrimination' among White employees will be reflected in lower job satisfaction where there are minorities and a demand for compensating wage increase. The evidence for White women employees was less clear. Interestingly, the posited routes that might explain such tastes – concerns about job insecurity or racialised tensions at the workplace – were not found in this study.

Employment opportunity and location

Location can be considered important in influencing employment experiences and opportunities in a number of ways. It can affect chances for different ethnic groups through differential employment rates (Owen, 1997). Either the fact of living in an area of high unemployment could be important, or the risks of unemployment could vary between groups with the composition of the area. There is limited evidence for the existence of 'neighbourhood effects' in Britain for the population as a whole. That is, that who lives near you matters in addition to your own characteristics for your life chances (Buck, 2001). Studies have also considered the labour markets in particular areas of the UK that have highly diverse populations in terms of ethnicity, and have found variation within them according to ethnic group, but also some variation between those of the same ethnicity living in such areas and living elsewhere (Owen and Johnson, 1996; Storkey and Lewis, 1996; Spence, 2005). Differential neighbourhood effects for ethnic groups were also found at the sub-regional level for which the Census enabled analysis (Clark and Drinkwater, 2007).

People can be tied into particular locations through housing or through kinship and local networks (Daley, 1998). Alternatively, particular locations may provide employment opportunities – through making the most of such local networks, through enabling the provision of 'niche' markets or through opportunities for entrepreneurship (self-employment) and the servicing of local markets. It has been argued that 'ethnic enclaves' may have advantages for those who live in them, or, alternatively, they may have negative effects (Galster, Metzger and Waite, 1999; Clark and Drinkwater, 2002). One of the posited advantages is the opportunity for self-employment. Research on self-employment shows that, while it may be a choice for some, it is often a route of last resort. For minority ethnic groups, self-employment can be a response to lack of opportunities and represent a 'constraint' rather than a choice (Clark and Drinkwater, 1998; Clark and Drinkwater, 2000). Thus, self-employment does not necessarily take place within the areas where minority ethnic groups themselves live, and the economic benefits of co-location are at best ambiguous (Clark and Drinkwater, 2002). Indeed, the authors identified no positive labour market outcomes associated with living in an 'enclave'. There may, of course, be other important benefits from living in proximity to those from the same ethnic group, including protection from racial harassment, social opportunities (Alam and Husband, 2006; Platt, 2006a) and access to specialised goods and services (Daley, 1998).

The UK's minority ethnic groups have distinctive migration histories (Al-Rasheed, 1996; Ballard, 1996b; Chance, 1996; Cheng, 1996; Daley, 1996; Eade et al, 1996; Owen, 1996a, 1996b; Peach, 1996b; Robinson, 1996a; Modood et al, 1997; Parekh, 2000; Hickman, 2005). These have intersected with changes in the economy and industry that have caused particular patterns of migration and settlement among previous (Peach and Rossiter, 1996) and more recent (Kyambi, 2005) immigrants, which have also been shaped by housing access and tenure, competition in housing and discriminatory housing markets (Dorling, 1997; Howes and Mullins, 1997; Phillips, 1997; Ratcliffe, 1997). It has been argued that race relations legislation of the late 1960s and mid-1970s was insufficient to counteract the housing and residential patterns that had become established, particularly when they were reinforced by the decline of manufacturing and processes of deindustrialisation, which further limited the mobility of those already living in the inner cities. These patterns were to have long-term effects on patterns of minority ethnic groups' settlement and for their outcomes (Phillips, 1998); although there is some evidence of differences in spatial distribution between immigrants and the 'second' (UK-born) generation (Robinson, 1996b). Although minority ethnic group concentrations in Britain are far from the levels associated with US 'ghettos' (Peach, 1996c), there has also been recent debate about whether spatial segregation is increasing – although that stems partly from a confusion between population growth and internal migration. Studies have indicated that minority ethnic groups tend to disperse from (rather than head towards) initial centres of concentration (that are often also areas of high deprivation) over time, in line with expressed desires and with more general moves towards suburbanisation (Simpson, 2005); see also Daley (1998); Dorsett (1998). New immigrants, may, however, have little option but to move into such areas initially – and, indeed, there may be clear benefits associated with doing so (Simpson, 2005).

Minority ethnic group perceptions of areas that were highly deprived on 'objective' criteria were found to be much more positive than majority views of less deprived areas (Bajekal et al, 2004). This finding may reflect the benefits of access to (although not numerical dominance of) members of the same ethnic group and the social and supportive resources they can offer (see also Platt, 2006a), even as other downsides of deprived areas were recognised.

Somewhere in between a 'preference' and a 'constraint' in relation to aspects of residential area is the role of racial harassment – either the experience of harassment or the fear of it. According to the 2005 Citizenship Survey, as many as one in five minority ethnic group members were 'very worried' about being attacked on the grounds of their ethnic origin (Kitchen et al, 2006). This can importantly affect the experience of an area and may well make relative concentrations of people from the same ethnic group more attractive than the area's other characteristics might warrant. However, the exact relationship between area, ethnicity and disadvantage is still not clear cut.

Different areas may suffer from different susceptibilities to changes in the economy and the shocks of recessions. To the extent that different groups are more or less concentrated in areas vulnerable to economic downturns, they may be more likely to suffer from unemployment (although see Iganski and Payne, 1999). It has been argued that minority ethnic groups' employment rates follow hypercyclical patterns (Modood, 1997b). That is, minority ethnic groups' unemployment rises faster than that of the White majority in times of recession and drops faster during an economic boom. While such effects might be attributable in part to the behaviour of employers, they may also be a consequence of patterns of residence. However, the existence of such hypercyclical patterns has been challenged, especially for more recent years (Leslie and Lindley, 2001). Instead, it has been argued that there was a partial hypercyclical effect, especially for some groups, notably Pakistanis and Bangladeshis (Lindley, 2005). That is, while minority ethnic groups' unemployment rose in recession, it failed to recover in economic upturn. This is consistent – at a group level – with the concept of the 'scarring' effects of unemployment and the impact of longer unemployment durations for those in employment.

However, Fieldhouse and Gould (1998) did not find that it was unemployment rates in areas of ethnic group concentration that accounted for minority ethnic groups' employment disadvantage. And Heath (2001), from his reading of Fieldhouse (1999), concluded that there was little support for spatial mismatch theories, that is, that where minority ethnic groups lived were areas of fewer job opportunities. By contrast, Owen and Green (2000) found a mismatch between jobs available in areas of minority ethnic concentrations and the match of these jobs to the skills of those living there.

The issue of accessibility of jobs, including access to transport and public transport infrastructure, has also been considered in reflecting on the role of residential location. Owen and Green (2000) found that all the 1991 Census minority ethnic groups were more likely to use public transport to get to work than the White group. Women from all groups were more reliant on public transport than men from the same group; but all minority ethnic group men had greater rates of public transport use than White women.

Location can also be linked to the type of occupation engaged in. Occupational segregation can be influenced by and influence geographical location (Rees and Phillips, 1996). There are clear patterns of occupational specialisation and segregation across different ethnic groups (Sly et al. 1998). And Chau and Yu (2001) have argued that the occupational segregation (or specialisation) of the Chinese in distribution and catering industries is the cause of their geographical dispersion, and results in greater isolation. On the other hand, occupational segregation may constrain people to live grouped near employment opportunities; or, conversely, geographical concentration may support ongoing occupational segregation in particular highly specific industries, such as the 'curry houses' of the East End and Birmingham (Carey, 2004). However, levels of occupational segregation are declining, alongside structural changes in the labour market (Blackwell and Guinea-Martin, 2005). Whether the jobs that people or groups were previously concentrated in are in 'growth' or 'declining' industries then becomes an important issue (Green, 1997). Owen and Green (2000, p 602) have argued that 'many people are in the 'wrong places' to benefit most from net employment growth', giving support to spatial mismatch theory.

It has been argued that relative concentration represents a positive choice, where a 'taste for isolation' is satisfied at the expense of economic advantage (Battu et al, 2005); see also Blackaby et al (2005). Battu et al (2005) argued that this can help to explain the poorer labour market outcomes of Pakistanis and Bangladeshis. The argument assumes that loss of cultural distinctiveness is the necessary price for economic assimilation, and that social/cultural integration leads to better economic outcomes. But Chau and Yu (2001) have challenged 'common sense' understandings of self-sufficiency or self-isolation. They point out that economic success may come at the cost of some social isolation. Equally, economic success may also facilitate patterns of residence in relative co-ethnic concentration combined with relative prosperity (Dorsett, 1998). And, as discussed above, the evidence is that movement away from concentrations occurs over time. Moreover, patterns of White 'self-isolation' in affluent areas are rarely investigated as representing a sacrifice of economic outcomes to 'cultural' preferences.

If geographical and occupational segregation tend to be associated with disadvantage, desegregation and 'social assimilation' do not necessarily result in the elimination of disadvantage. As Peach (2005, p 201) points out, 'Caribbean segregation levels are moderate and decreasing. Social intermixture is significant and rising'. But 'while the Caribbean population is economically disadvantaged but increasingly socially assimilated, the Indian population is generally economically advantaged but has retained its social distinctiveness' (Peach, 2005, p 200) and that 'social distinctiveness' does seem to imply a preference for locating near other Indians (Dorsett, 1998).

Notes

[1] In the latter case, a large qualitative study of transnational Jamaicans suggests that it is possible that different measures of what constitutes a 'successful' outcome may make a difference, with a 'good working-class' job being a measure of success for first-generation Caribbeans, especially if coming from impoverished backgrounds (Platt and Thompson, 2006).

[2] This source is one example where the data are outside the period of the review but the study has nevertheless been included. This is justified on the grounds that it is an important issue that the study covers, the study is a strong one and there is nothing comparable (or no comparable source) that falls within the period of the review.

SIX

Family structure and kinship

Family structure and patterns of household formation can be related to poverty in a number of ways. Larger households can include a larger number of potential earners as well as more mouths to feed. In families with children, particularly young children, the mother is more likely to be economically inactive – or to be working part time, with the lower rates of remuneration that typically go with such work. And families with large numbers of children are more likely to be in poverty than those with fewer. But lone-parent households, which tend to be smaller, have very high risks of poverty. Older people can create demands on household income, but they can also bring in pensions and other assets, as well as potentially serving as sources of childcare, thus facilitating parents', or rather mothers', labour market participation. Larger households may put pressure on housing and create associated problems of housing deprivation, such as overcrowding; while the relative costs of housing and of maintenance will be that much greater for smaller households.

The structure and characteristics of households (or, more commonly, the immediate family unit or benefit unit) as well as the sources of income within them will also affect benefit entitlement. Thus, means-testing may mean that the impact of unemployment on one partner may raise questions about whether it is worthwhile for the other partner to work. The presence of dependent children will create eligibility for child benefit; but the presence of non-dependent children in work may reduce Housing Benefit payments.

To the extent that these forms of household structure vary by ethnicity, so will the associated risks of poverty vary with ethnic group. However, risks of particular circumstances are not necessarily equal across groups. Even in those situations that bring increased risks of poverty for all (workless households, households with a disabled adult, lone-parent families) there remain substantial differences between ethnic groups, with heightened risks for the most disadvantaged, typically Pakistani and Bangladeshi households (Platt, 2006f). Conversely, research has also identified that the high relative risks of poor outcomes associated with teenage pregnancy compared to later childbirth in the population as a whole do not hold for those groups where early marriage and childbirth is more common (Robson and Berthoud, 2003).

There are particular ways in which household formation intersects with ethnicity to create heightened or reduced risks. An obvious example is the intersection of the benefit system with immigration status and its impact on household arrangements, discussed further in Chapter Seven. Thus, family members who have recently arrived on the basis of family reunification are required to have 'no recourse to public funds' until they acquire settled status. In such circumstances, living independently may not be an option but living together will increase demands on household resources (Evandrou, 2000). Thus, large households can act as a protection against (severe) poverty as well as contributing towards the risk of it. And disentangling the strategies that may be being used to maximise family welfare is not straightforward.

Berrington (1994) noted the different demographic patterns of minority ethnic groups compared to the majority: younger, with a different balance between men and women, and also with differences in levels of fertility and age at marriage. Analysis of the 2001 Census showed substantial variation by ethnic group and religious affiliation in relation to household structure and family type (Connolly and Raha, 2006). Pakistani and Bangladeshi households were most likely to be multi-family (23% and 24%, respectively), and least likely to be one-person households (12% and 9%, respectively). One in five Black African households were also multi-family, but a sizeable share of Black African households were single-person households (30%). Bangladeshi households were largest overall, averaging 4.5 persons, followed by Pakistani (4.1 persons) and Indian (3.3 persons) households. The overall average household size was 2.3 persons.

Approximately half of Other Black and Black Caribbean and just over a third of Black African households were lone-parent households (compared to 10% of households overall consisting of a lone parent with dependent children). There was also variation by ethnic group in the extent to which lone-parent households stemmed from divorce or separation or did not involve marriage. There is thus substantial variation in the extent to which different groups are exposed to the poverty risks associated with either larger household sizes or lone-parent families.

There is also evidence that family form and related poverty risks vary substantially with ethnic group. Recent analysis of the Families and Children Study showed the overrepresentation of mothers from Black groups in the bottom quintile of the income distribution, with 35% of them in the bottom 20% of incomes compared to 20% of mothers from one of the South Asian groups and 16% of White mothers (Lyon et al, 2006). This result could be linked to the fact that 54% of the Black mothers were lone parents compared to 25% of the White mothers and 14% of the Asian mothers. However, the small numbers and the consequent high level of aggregation of disparate ethnic groups does not allow more detailed consideration of this issue in this source. However, it is consistent with Berthoud's earlier, but much more detailed analysis carried out on family formation (Berthoud, 2005).

Analysis of the Family Resources Survey showed that families with larger numbers of children have higher risks of poverty (Bradshaw et al, 2006; Iacovou and Berthoud, 2006). This was true even when other relevant factors associated with poverty were controlled (Bradshaw et al, 2006). The greater risks of poverty were due to lower earning probabilities of parents in large families, lower wages, as well as the extra demands on family income created by larger numbers of children (Iacovou and Berthoud, 2006). These factors cannot necessarily be considered independently as larger families will reduce the extent to which working or working extra hours can lift a family out of poverty. Over a quarter of Bangladeshi families, nearly a fifth of Pakistani families and nearly one in ten Black African families have four or more children. The risks of having a large family are significantly greater for African families than White families, once the mother's age at first birth and parents' qualifications (themselves significant influences on family size) are taken into account; while separate analysis of Pakistani and Bangladeshi families showed that family size was largely determined by the age at which the mother started having children; and that the negative relationship between parental qualifications and family size was also particularly strong for families from these groups (Iacovou and Berthoud, 2006). Nevertheless, risks of poverty among Pakistani and Bangladeshi families remained greater even taking account of family size (Bradshaw et al, 2006). Thus, larger families may contribute to differential risks of poverty but cannot explain them.

The reasons for these differences are various: we can consider the impact of immigration processes and their legacy, the role of cultural beliefs relating to family life and participation in work, and the constraints posed by limited opportunities and lack of support and responses to such constraints.

The extent to which age and sex distributions and patterns of family structure are a consequence of immigration patterns varies across groups (Bosveld and Connolly, 2006). The stereotypical immigration narrative is of younger men migrating and being subsequently joined by wives, often younger, and by other family members or more distant kin in processes of chain migration. These processes can be exacerbated by changes in immigration policy. For example, the introduction of immigration controls on commonwealth citizens in 1962 increased family reunification for some groups while leading to particular patterns of chain migration concentrated around particular industries in others. However, migration is no longer predominantly undertaken by men, so the profile of new migrants is rather different – and for some groups, such as among Caribbeans, women's economic migration occurred alongside men's from the start. Moreover, forced migration results in rather different patterns of family entry and settlement, with whole families sometimes moving together. In addition, the initial distinctive sex ratios and age structures will tend to shift over time, as the first generation ages and subsequent generations are no longer so subject to the restrictions and constraints associated with migration (Bosveld and Connolly, 2006).

Nevertheless, the age profiles of Britain's different ethnic groups remain relatively distinct. These aspects of demography and the extent of locally resident kin influence family patterns and life stages of Britain's ethnic groups.

Cultural and religious influences on differences in lifestyles are often considered in relation to both family forms and women's economic inactivity rates, although the separation of the 'cultural' in this way is not unproblematic (Anthias, 2001).

Marriage on its own was much more likely to reduce economic activity for Pakistani and Bangladeshi women than for Caribbean and White women (Bhopal, 1998; Dale et al, 2006). Having children reduced economic activity of women across the board; but there were still differences between ethnic groups, with Pakistani and Bangladeshi women least likely to combine motherhood with paid work and Caribbean women most likely to (Dale et al, 2006). The Caribbean 'norm' of combining motherhood and paid work has been explored in more depth in a qualitative study of 20 Caribbean mothers, where it was found to be both a source of strength but also bringing pressures and tensions with it (Reynolds, 2001).

The Families and Children Study revealed that mothers with children from aggregated Black and South Asian groups were more likely to have no qualifications and/or to have a partner with no qualifications than their White counterparts (Lyon et al, 2006). This is broadly consistent with levels of qualifications in the population as a whole discussed above. However, women from these minority ethnic groups were also more likely to have higher qualifications and a more highly qualified partner, which suggests differences in the way qualifications relate to probability of motherhood across groups, with family being apparently a lower priority for more highly educated White women. A study of Muslim women undergraduates found that a strong commitment to family life was expressed alongside a commitment to paid work – and the freedom to choose (Tyrer and Ahmad, 2006). In this study, the potential benefits to the next generation of having an aspirational and highly qualified mother who was in a position of full-time care were identified. This perspective is consistent with evidence on the importance of mother's education to children's subsequent outcomes.

Evidence for cultural or religious influences on labour market participation and family life is hard to disentangle from the constraints that may also lead to particular family patterns. For example, high unemployment rates afflict Bangladeshi women who also have low rates of labour market participation. We already know that in general women's probability of defining themselves as inactive (rather than unemployed) increases with the time spent unemployed, and this is generally regarded as an adaptive response. Moreover, not only lack of employment, but lack of appropriate employment, which suits skills and can be combined with caring responsibilities, is likely to be a major issue. Pakistani and Bangladeshi women may have different priorities in relation to the balance of work and family (Dale, 2002), but the complexity of demands of bringing up children on a low income may also play an important role, particularly if other caring responsibilities are involved as well (Salway et al, 2007).

The issue of appropriate childcare has been highlighted as an issue in minority ethnic group women's labour market participation. And the lack of available grandparents to provide support in childcare has been highlighted for the Indian group, specifically (Craig, 2005). Notions of the 'extended family' that 'looks after its own' both in relation to children and elder care have been extensively refuted by research revealing the isolation of some older people and lack of access to social care and related forms of support (Boneham, 1997). Nevertheless, such stereotypes appear to retain a strong hold, affecting the extent to which those from marginalised groups may be forced to utilise local links and resources to 'fill the gap' (Zetter et al, 2006).

The interaction between (views on) motherhood and family, including size of family, educational qualifications and ethnicity are clearly complex, and are likely to become more so, as both levels of qualifications and employment patterns of minority ethnic group women shift over generations, and with these shifts the ways in which expectations are shaped. Increasingly, attention is being paid to the specific experiences of minority ethnic group and Muslim women, both in education, especially higher education (Ahmad, 2001; Ahmad et al, 2003), and in employment, including the combination of family and employment (Dale, 2002; Botcherby, 2006; Peach, 2006). There is also a focus on younger women's (and their families') educational and employment aspirations (Bhavnani, 2006), which have been shown as being maintained in the face of stereotyping approaches of careers advisers and teachers (Basit, 1996, 1997; Tyrer and Ahmad, 2006). Aspirations among women in employment and their variation by ethnic group have also been addressed in a specific survey conducted by the Equal Opportunities Commission (Botcherby, 2006). This revealed how comparable aspirations tended to be across women from the four groups considered (White, Pakistani, Bangladeshi and Black Caribbean). These various studies show the diversity of views and experiences as well as highlighting the individual agency of the women concerned. They both act as a check on culturalist explanations, but also show how the interaction of aspirations (own and others'), group and societal norms, the demands of family care, and structural and discriminatory obstacles to employment create complex patterns of economic activity and family life and ways of describing them.

Moreover, patterns of household structure and formation are not fixed. Indicators of change are increases in age of marriage, in prevalence of cohabitation and in interethnic unions and decreases in number of children and age at first birth. For example, births to women under the age of 20 have been falling among the South Asian groups (Berthoud, 2001). Studies of interethnic unions have shown that they vary substantially in their prevalence by sex and ethnic group, being least common among the White majority. Nevertheless, they are still on the increase. Rates of interethnic unions in England, according to the 2001 Census amounted to 7% of all unions (Berrington, 1996; Berthoud, 2005; DMAG, 2005; Peach, 2005).

Of course, intermarriage does not imply economic integration, nor should it be regarded as a prerequisite for it (Coleman, 1994), but it is one indicator of the extent to which there is dispersion in patterns of family formation and household structure. It should be set aside other shifts, such as older age of marriage in younger generations of minority ethnic groups (Berrington, 1994), greater engagement with the labour market and access to professional occupations among younger, second-generation Pakistani and Bangladeshi women (Basit,

1996; Bhopal, 1998; Dale, 2002), as well as the increased tendency for single parenthood among UK-born Caribbean women (Berthoud, 2005), and the tendency towards delayed childrearing among White women (particularly those with higher qualifications).

Overall, then, demographic patterns and family structure have a role in the different poverty risks of different ethnic groups. However, there are complex patterns of cause and effect. Change over time further complicates the implications for policy. The contribution of family form nevertheless remains of importance to both effective analysis of poverty risks and to the development of appropriate income maintenance strategies to reduce poverty and poverty differentials.

SEVEN

Access to and use of social security benefits

As well as employment income, Chapters One, Three and Four identified benefit income as a source of income that impacts on whether or not a household is in poverty.[1] The amount of income from benefits that goes into a household will depend on eligibility, take-up and the extent to which the benefit is administered accurately and fairly. (For a fuller discussion of the relationship between ethnicity and social security, see Law, 1996: chapter 2; Craig, 1999; Platt, 2002: chapter 6, 2003c.) This chapter briefly considers these three areas and their potential impact on social security income in households of different ethnic groups.

Eligibility is influenced by such factors as household form (discussed in Chapter Six), accumulation of National Insurance credits, other sources of income, belonging to the relevant category (for example, child, over 60), immigration status, and evaluations of meeting the relevant criteria, for example for disability benefits.

Take-up is influenced by the costs of the claiming relative to the benefits, where costs may involve 'stigma' as well as time and energy. It is also influenced by having relevant information and by perceptions of eligibility or probability of making a successful claim. Furthermore, some benefits are subject to lower levels of take-up overall than others. For example, the takeup of Disability Living Allowance is estimated to be between 30% and 50% for the care component and between 50% and 70% for the mobility component (Craig and Greenslade, 1998), although accurate assessments for disability benefits are hard to establish given the complex criteria for awarding them. Pension Credit also faces relatively low rates of take-up, whereas take-up of Housing Benefit and Income Support is typically high. To the extent that particular ethnic groups are overrepresented among those eligible for benefits for which establishing eligibility is problematic or which are subject to low take-up, they are more at risk of eligible non-receipt. Contributory benefits are less subject to stigma and may have better rates of take-up, other things being equal, than non-contributory benefits.

Issues of equitable administration have the potential for impacting on claimants more the higher the degree of discretion there is for decision makers. Thus, they may be more relevant to areas such as the Social Fund than to, say, Income Support payments. Decisions made by those outside the benefits system may also be relevant here: for example, doctors play an important role in enabling patients to access Incapacity Benefit, and despite proposed changes to sickness and disability benefits (DWP, 2006a), their 'gatekeeper' role is likely to remain in some form.

Eligibility

Eligibility for insurance benefits, including pensions, is of course based on a record of National Insurance contributions. Interrupted – or non-existent – work histories will impact more heavily on pension rights for those groups with high rates of economic inactivity and unemployment (as have been described in earlier chapters of this book) as well as on their entitlement to Incapacity Benefit and contributions-based Jobseeker's Allowance. Levels of savings and alternative income sources determine eligibility for means-tested benefits, including tax credits, additionally to any other criteria. Household composition (also discussed in Chapter Six) may have an effect on actual or assumed incomes for some benefits, as well as, clearly, on categorical criteria for eligibility.

Eligibility for means-tested benefits is dependent on residence status. This means that for some newly immigrated subject to limitations on 'recourse to public funds' or those with work-related entry rights, rights to claim may be limited or unclear. Bloch (1997) identified a number of ways in which benefit rules themselves can disadvantage those from particular ethnic groups. Residence requirements can affect those who have spent or spend substantial periods of time abroad. Where people have geographically distant ties, they may choose, or be obliged, to spend substantial periods away from Britain. There may also be problems in the interpretation and application of the 'habitual residence test'. This provision requires a judgement about whether someone is 'habitually resident' and there is substantial evidence to show that it tends to be operated inappropriately, and that the recourse to it is a result of racist stereotyping and assumptions (National Association of Citizens Advice Bureaux, 1996; CPAG, 2002).

Take-up

There is little work on differential rates of benefit take-up by ethnicity (House of Commons Work and Pensions Committee, 2005). Work by the Disability Alliance indicated that there may be underclaiming of Disability Living Allowance by minority ethnic groups (Wayne, 2003), and the House of Commons Work and Pensions Committee (2005) stressed the importance of improving the knowledge base in this area. Preliminary work from the Department for Work and Pensions indicated ethnic differences in the take-up of certain benefits (Platt, 2006f). Analysis of differential use of disability benefits among those with a long-term illness has also provided prima facie evidence of differences in take-up propensities (Salway et al, 2007).

Bloch (1993) stressed the importance of information in appropriate languages in access to and take-up of social security among minority ethnic groups. However, the effectiveness of a focus on language and translation to facilitate take-up has been questioned (Gordon et al, 2002). Law et al (1994) discussed the relevance of attitudes, cultural considerations and perceived justifications for claiming. The authors found that Chinese respondents were particularly sensitive to the stigma of benefit claiming. The implication of this is that there may be a small group of very poor Chinese people, who are not receiving benefit entitlement. Attitudes to stigma among Bangladeshi Muslims were more various, with some stress on the right to claim benefit entitlement.

Attitudes to claiming were also found to be one of a number of relevant 'barriers' in a study of barriers to claiming means-tested state support among older people from seven different minority ethnic groups (Barnard and Pettigrew, 2003). The study, which covered Indian, Bangladeshi, Pakistani, Chinese, African, African Caribbean and Irish elders, identified some barriers that were specific to certain minority ethnic groups: language issues, lack of a National Insurance number (among South Asian older women) and concerns about the impact of claiming on residence status. Lack of knowledge of the system and fears about engaging with it (an issue also raised by Gordon et al, 2002) along with literacy problems were identified as general issues in take-up but which were enhanced for minority ethnic groups. Some barriers were identified that were associated with lower take-up across older people, rather than concerning minority ethnic groups in particular: these included the arduous nature of the claims process. In addition, Bloch (1997) found that where benefits have been in payment but the claimant is absent for a period the family may not claim the support due. And, as mentioned, means-tested benefits already come with a stigma attached. If that stigma is combined with assumptions relating to the ethnicity of the claimant the whole application procedure may become intolerable (Cohen et al, 1992).

Administration

There is little direct evidence on how the administration of benefits does or may affect receipt among different ethnic groups. However, income-related benefits tend to require more complex procedures and the production of more 'evidence'. Disability benefits also present particular hurdles in terms of assessment (Salway et al, 2007). Whether these affect groups differentially, however, is not clearly known. Simpson (1991) suggested that the practice of requests for passports or other 'excessive demands for evidence' was an issue for claimants from minority ethnic groups. Such requests, if they cannot be met, may result in benefit being withheld and consequent hardship.

Overall, then, there are some suggestions that certain ethnic groups may have greater difficulty accessing benefit income than others. But there is little hard evidence in this area. Differences in the use of benefits and of take-up certainly warrant further attention.

Note

[1] As mentioned above (p 59), the third domain of income from assets and savings does not invoke issues independent of those covered in Chapter Five and this chapter and so is not separately considered.

Part Four
Implications

This Part considers the implications of the discussion and findings summarised in this review. In Chapter Eight, the implications for policy of what we already know about ethnicity and poverty are highlighted, with a focus on employment and income maintenance policies; while in Chapter Nine gaps in research are identified with the consequent implications for a future research agenda.

EIGHT

Implications for policy

This book has touched on areas that relate to a number of policy agendas, for example those around 'community cohesion' (Home Office, 2004b, 2005a), now a responsibility of the Department for Communities & Local Government, social exclusion (HM Government, 2006), health inequalities (DH, 2003) and immigration policy (Home Office, 2005b).

The discussion in this chapter will, however, focus on the role of policies relating to employment (including tackling discrimination and harnessing skills) and to income maintenance for those of working age as well as for pensioners and children. Moreover, income from employment impacts on those of all ages, including those of pension age: life-time employment record and earnings affect the amount of pension income older people receive; and there are clear differences in the extent to which different ethnic groups have private pension provision (Ginn and Arber, 2000). In addition, pensioners do not necessarily live alone – and indeed, multi-generation households are much more common among Pakistani, Bangladeshi and Indian households. Thus, older people could benefit from, or suffer from, the extent to which those of working age in the same household are in (well-paid) employment. The discussion therefore relates to agendas on minority ethnic employment (Strategy Unit, 2003; Ethnic Minority Employment Task Force, 2005), child poverty (Harker, 2006) and monitoring of poverty and social exclusion (DWP, 2006b).

Employment-related policies

Lack of employment among working-age adults is an issue for poverty among minority ethnic groups. The Department for Work and Pensions has recognised this and has a strategy that acknowledges the importance of a number of relevant areas. It also has a Public Service Agreement target to reduce the employment gap between the minority and majority populations. As well as targeted attention to the employment of minority ethnic groups there are a number of generally applicable policy areas that have particular relevance to the employment of specific ethnic groups.

General policies that are of relevance to minority ethnic employment rates and that have already found a place on the policy agenda to a greater or lesser extent, include:

- appropriate, accessible and affordable childcare;
- supporting people with health problems to remain in and return to work;

- the National Minimum Wage;
- helping young people and the long-term unemployed into work, including through developing skills;
- the Work Search Premium for partners in non-working households.

While specific approaches include:

- the recognition of and attempts to combat employer discrimination;
- attention to the promotion of race equality through the public sector procurement process (IRIS Consulting, 2005);
- the introduction of Partner's Outreach for those non-working, minority ethnic partners living in low-income households in particular areas (DWP, 2006b).

There has also been a recent recognition of the importance of linking the employment and child poverty agendas (Platt, 2006f).

These policy agendas and initiatives are to be welcomed as according with the pressing differences in unemployment and in workless households between groups. From the evidence of this book, however, it is clear that there is much still to be done. The following paragraphs indicate a number of areas that could be strengthened or developed.

One area that is acknowledged at the policy level, but which the findings of this book indicate needs emphasis, is the role of employer discrimination. This is clearly on the agenda, but a more developed understanding of where and how it operates (including through the use of administrative Jobcentre Plus information) and the development of strategies to address it should be a high priority. This is also likely to have an effect on the opportunities that are available and that are perceived as being options by minority ethnic group members. The obstacles posed to progression by discrimination within employment as well as to employment also need to be addressed.

Decreasing the employment differential between the minority and majority populations is important, but only part of the story. There are two points here. First, aggregating minority ethnic groups may not be the most effective form of target. Patterns of employment, unemployment and inactivity vary across groups and between men and women both within and across groups. The constraints are also gendered and the relationship between work and family life is typically highly gendered. The employment agenda also needs to recognise how, despite apparently declining sex segregation, labour markets and opportunities as well as barriers to employment are different for men and women from different ethnic groups. Second, the target should not recognise entry into employment as the endpoint of the policy but consideration should be given to what job. It is not just getting a job but what sort of a job – and how long it is likely to last – that is important. Policy attention needs to be focused more clearly on job quality and retention, and the possibilities for career progression, as well as continuing to pursue a 'making work pay' agenda. We saw that levels of pay in employment can mean that households from certain ethnic groups with an adult in employment and dependent children still have high risks of poverty.

In relation to making work pay, the rates of the National Minimum Wage and its enforcement are relevant issues, and should continue to receive scrutiny and evaluation. The rate of pay for part-time work is also an issue that affects some groups more than others. Equalising terms and conditions of part-time compared to full-time pay is only one part of this: given the very different jobs that are available part time compared to full time, flexibility within employment, which allows reduction of hours when circumstances (for example, caring responsibilities or health status) require it, is important for maintaining reasonable levels of pay alongside part-time hours.

Part of the emphasis on the quality of the job and job retention will relate to the skills agenda. Here the employment agenda links with schooling, post-compulsory education and the development of lifetime skills. As has been noted, there is evidence of clear motivation towards education among minority ethnic groups. However, there are substantial differences in educational qualifications by ethnic group by the end of compulsory schooling – and the impacts of 'catching up' later – by staying on longer for the same level of qualifications, on own and households' poverty rates needs to be given due attention. Education Maintenance Allowances, after all, only last until the age of 18. There may be an argument for continuing them for longer as a short-term policy, while the longer-term goal should be to create more equal outcomes within the compulsory school period. While this is the espoused goal of policy, the moves towards greater school independence and 'parental' choice (DfES, 2005b) may, arguably, make more equal outcomes harder to achieve (Jenkins et al, 2006).

For those in search of work, the conversion of existing skills and the recognition of experience and qualifications obtained abroad seems to be an issue for both employers and employment advisers. This links to the importance of finding stable and appropriate – rather than any – work. Providing adequate support within the new job, for those with a sustained period out of the labour market or who are changing sector or type of job, and assisting employers to provide flexible arrangements where needed may also be important (particularly in relation to caring responsibilities – both for children and for family members).

The role of state benefits

As has been noted throughout the book, earnings are only one component of household income. State benefits have an important role to play, and this extends to the benefits that are or are not received by all members of the household in which a given individual at risk of poverty is living. For example, the extent of pension income affects not just pensioners but the household income of those with whom they are living. Despite the lack of systematic studies of ethnicity and take-up, the available evidence suggests that minority ethnic groups both experience more limited entitlement to certain benefits (through, for example, interrupted contributions records) and are less likely to claim various forms of benefit to which they are entitled. Thus, ensuring take-up among the eligible is an important area for policy.

In addition, a higher level of financial remuneration for those who take on caring responsibilities for the long-term sick could have positive effects on poverty rates, particularly in families with children, and facilitate the combination of such caring with childcare, arguably promoting better welfare consequences for the family in certain circumstances than attempting to place the 'carer' in paid employment.

Tax credits generally mean that those working only relatively small numbers of hours can expect themselves and their families to be better off than those in receipt of (other) means-tested benefits. However, 'marginal tax rates' tend to be particularly high for those on Housing Benefit, and the levels of rent in London, where a very large proportion of minority ethnic group members live, make this a particular issue. The move to local housing allowances may assist families in the private rented sector in this respect, but not those in the local authority sector. Understanding of eligibility for Housing Benefit in work has been found to be poor (Turley and Thomas, 2006); and for those living in complex households the issues around balancing gains through pay and tax credits against losses in Housing Benefit may be particularly complex or confusing. It needs to be recognised that risks of loss of assured income or instability in income sources may be felt as more problematic than the potential gains in income. The problem of balancing out housing costs against potential rewards from work, and improving claimants' understanding of the issues, is worthy of continued attention.

NINE

Implications for research

Despite the wealth of high-quality research on ethnic differences and experiences across a wide range of areas, gaps still remain in our knowledge and understanding. This chapter briefly outlines a few areas that would benefit from investigation, how that might be pursued and the possible shape of a future research agenda. It highlights six broad areas where further research or development of existing approaches would be beneficial. These areas of research do not simply represent areas of academic concern but are crucial to how the problem of differences in poverty among different ethnic groups is framed and how policy responses are shaped and formulated. Further research in certain areas is necessary if policy is to be able to respond appropriately and effectively to the major challenge of ethnic (and religious) differences in poverty, and in child poverty in particular.

First, there are gaps in the amount we know about poverty and ethnicity and its details. Specifically, we could benefit from up-to-date and more detailed information on poverty rates within households of different types, on composition of incomes within households and how these vary among poor and non-poor households from different ethnic groups, depth (severity of poverty), and durations and dynamics of poverty experience. The following points consider these issues in more detail:

- Household poverty levels: variation and composition

To get a grasp on the relative contribution of the different contributory factors in poverty rates by ethnic group, it is important to know more about household income levels and have a more detailed understanding of variation according to household characteristics across and within groups. In addition, research analysing the different sources of income contributing to household income, which family members they originate from, and how this varies by ethnic group, would allow more understanding of sources of poverty and policy implications.

Such analysis could also be complemented by analysis of expenditure and by investigation of inter-household transfers. These would provide a greater insight into the use that is made of incomes and the welfare resulting from them. While this further agenda is not very likely with existing quantitative sources, it could benefit from qualitative approaches to understanding different meanings and understandings of poverty. Subjective understandings of poverty are likely to play an important role in how people respond to and manage their circumstances and to the extent that particular initiatives are relevant to them. It may be possible to explore some of the issues around inter-household transfers and mutuality when the proposed new UK longitudinal survey with its ethnicity component comes on line (see www.esrcsocietytoday.ac.uk/)

• Poverty (and employment) dynamics and durations

Long-term poverty is acknowledged to be potentially a more serious issue than short–term poverty in terms of its effects. Longer as opposed to shorter periods of poverty can also be more detrimental at particular life stages, such as in childhood, where consequences may last well into the future. However, we have only limited evidence of variation in poverty durations by ethnicity. Similarly, there is little research on employment dynamics and durations. A more detailed understanding of poverty and employment dynamics by ethnic group would also be informative about levels of insecurity or instability. These areas are themselves increasingly being framed as policy issues in their own right. (See, for example, the Institute for Public Policy Research project on risk and resilience, www.ippr.org.) Ethnic differences in such insecurity and their responses to it would also enhance understandings of resilience and appropriate policy responses. Up until now there has been little in the way of data through which to analyse poverty dynamics and ethnicity. Current developments that will assist such work are the possible linking of claimant count cohort data to the Office for National Statistics Longitudinal Study, where large sample sizes and ethnic group information facilitate ethnicity analysis, and the proposed development of a large UK Household Longitudinal Survey with a specific ethnicity component to it (see www.esrcsocietytoday. ac.uk/). It will be a few years until the latter development is at a stage to enable analysis of change over time. Meanwhile, however, it might be worth exploring further the potential of existing sources to allow some indication of durations and dynamics.

• Depth and severity of poverty

Durations of poverty also relate to issues around severity of poverty and material deprivation. As noted, what evidence we have suggests that where the extent of poverty is greatest, the depth of poverty is also greater; however, the knowledge base is not extensive. Analysis of the pooled years of the Family Resources Survey could add measures of severity (such as the size of poverty gaps) to information measures of extent derived from this source. Analysis of material deprivation by ethnicity will also become increasingly possible as the number of years in which deprivation questions have been asked in the Family Resources Survey increases.

Second, we would do well to understand more about the use and take-up of particular benefits and their role in family incomes. This would build on the work on pensions cited above and would attempt to link that to issues of eligibility and non-take-up. There are clearly different issues relating to means-tested and non-means-tested benefits, but indicative research indicates that there may be issues around take-up or entitlement in both areas. The Department for Work and Pensions appears to be moving towards developing estimates of eligible non-take-up of means-tested benefits. This would be a welcome development, which would have a crucial role to play in informing approaches to take-up. There is also further work to be done around differential receipt of disability benefits and pensions to ascertain the extent to which this stems from ineligibility or non-take-up, and the extent to which eligibility requirements are appropriate.

Third, there are two areas of the labour market where knowledge could still be improved: quantifying employer discrimination and exploring the costs and benefits of self-employment for different ethnic groups.

- Identifying employer discrimination

All the evidence suggests that employer discrimination exists and plays a significant role in the 'ethnic penalty' experienced by members of minority ethnic groups; but the extent and processes by which it occurs are not so clear. Employer 'tests', such as those that were carried out in the 1970s and 1980s, would provide us with a much clearer measure of the extent of employer discrimination at job entry. Independent researchers (rather than government) would be best placed to repeat such studies. In addition, a detailed examination of cases put before tribunals would allow greater understanding of in-work discrimination, even if it could not provide an actual measure of extent. These investigations could be considered alongside existing self-reports of perceived discrimination in the survey literature to enhance our understanding of both the amount of discrimination and the routes by which it occurs.

There is also a role for investigating the relationship between racial discrimination and other forms of discrimination, for example that relating to disability. Attempting to understand such a relationship would be informative about the processes and impacts of discrimination. This would also link with the work of the Equalities Review (The Equalities Review, 2006) and of the Discrimination Law Review (see www.womenandequalityunit.gov.uk/dlr/index.htm).

- Self-employment incomes and experience

There are a small number of valuable studies of self-employment and ethnicity, and the relative role of choice and constraint in decisions to engage in self-employment, as discussed in the book. However, income and earnings analyses typically ignore those in self-employment, given the difficulties of accurately estimating income. The differences in rates of self-employment by ethnic group render this an important area for further investigation to understand its impact. The long hours associated with self-employment and its frequent involvement of other family members may also be important in considering its role in the family, its impact on child welfare and how it constrains the labour supply of other family members.

Fourth, despite some theoretical developments around notions of 'ethnic capital' and a strong current interest in the role of social capital and how to support it, we know relatively little about the role of ethnically based networks in enabling or inhibiting opportunities and social mobility, or about how levels of human capital within a group can contribute to an individual's life chances and to escaping poverty. A research agenda that tried to unpick some of the assumptions involved in discussions of social capital and empirically to analyse the nature of networks across and within ethnic groups and their properties could provide a valuable contribution to understanding how particular patterns of association can be productive (or protective) in different ways (Alam and Husband, 2006).

Fifth, there is much interest in understanding change across generations and the transmission of poverty (or breaks in transmission). There is, as noted above, a limited amount of work that explores intergenerational transmission of advantage in terms of class, and other studies that compare cohorts from earlier and later periods on a range of characteristics. However, the understanding of the ways in which material disadvantage in one generation shape the experiences of the subsequent generation, and ethnic similarities and differences in these influences and their intersection with other aspects of experience (such as family, locality and so on) would benefit from explicit investigation, possibly using histories from current cohorts of people from different ethnic groups.

Sixth, there remain challenges in understanding differences in experience between minority ethnic groups. We could benefit from furthering our understanding of why some routes out of/to avoid poverty work for some groups and not for others. Related to this is why the 'ethnic penalty' should be particularly salient for some groups and not for others. It is not clear why some groups manage to do better than their circumstances would suggest, and thus why risk factors vary across groups. And we do not have a clear understanding of how particular family forms may be protective against poverty. Thus, there may be a role for an in-depth approach to understanding differences within apparently similar contexts around these issues.

References

Ahmad, F. (2001) 'Modern traditions? British Muslim women and academic achievement', *Gender and Education*, 13(2), pp 137-52.

Ahmad, F., Modood, T. and Lissenburgh, S. (2003) *South Asian Women and Employment in Britain: The Interaction of Gender and Ethnicity*. London: PSI.

Al-Rasheed, M. (1996) 'The Other-Others: hidden Arabs?', in C. Peach (ed) *Ethnicity in the 1991 Census: Volume Two: The Ethnic Minority Populations of Great Britain*. London: HMSO, pp 206-20.

Alam, M.Y. and Husband, C. (2006) *British-Pakistani Men from Bradford: Linking Narratives to Policy*. York: Joseph Rowntree Foundation.

Alcock, P. (2006) *Understanding Poverty* (3rd edition). Basingstoke: Palgrave.

Amin, K. and Oppenheim, C. (1992) *Poverty in Black and White: Deprivation and Ethnic Minorities*. London: CPAG in association with the Runnymede Trust.

Anderson, B. (1991) *Imagined Communities: Reflections on the Origins and Spread of Nationalism*. London: Verso.

Ansari, H. (2002) *Muslims in Britain*. London: Minority Rights Group International.

Anthias, F. (2001) 'The concept of "social division" and theorising social stratification: looking at ethnicity and class', *Sociology*, 35(4), pp 835-54.

Aspinall, P. (2001) 'Operationalising the collection of ethnicity data in studies of the sociology of health and illness', *Sociology of Health and Illness*, 23(6), pp 829-62.

Bajekal, M., Blane, D., Grewal, I., Karlsen, S. and Nazroo, J. (2004) 'Ethnic differences in influences on quality of life at older ages: a quantitative analysis', *Ageing and Society*, 24, pp 709-28.

Baker, M. and Benjamin, D. (1997) 'The role of the family in immigrants' labor-market activity: an evaluation of alternative explanations', *American Economic Review*, 87, pp 705-27.

Ballard, R. (1996a) 'Negotiating race and ethnicity: exploring the implications of the 1991 Census', *Patterns of Prejudice*, 30(3), pp 3-34.

Ballard, R. (1996b) 'The Pakistanis: stability and introspection', in C. Peach (ed) *Ethnicity in the 1991 Census: Volume Two: The Ethnic Minority Populations of Great Britain*. London: HMSO, pp 121-49.

Banton, M. (1997) *Ethnic and Racial Consciousnes* (2nd edition). London: Longman.

Banton, M. (1998) *Racial Theories*. Cambridge: Cambridge University Press.

Barnard, H. and Pettigrew, N. (2003) *Delivering Benefits and Services for Black and Minority Ethnic Older People*. Leeds: Corporate Document Services (www.dwp.gov.uk/asd/asd5/summ2003-2004/201summ.pdf).

Barnes, H. (2006) *Proposals for Pension Reform: Implications for Black and Minority Ethnic Communities*. London: Runnymede.

Bartley, M. and Plewis, I. (1997) 'Does health-selective mobility account for socioeconomic differences in health? Evidence from England and Wales 1971 to 1991', *Journal of Health and Social Behavior*, 38(4), pp 376-86.

Barth, F. (1969) *Ethnic Groups and Boundaries: The Social Organisation of Culture Difference*. London: Allen & Unwin.

Basit, T.N. (1996) 'I'd hate to be just a housewife: career aspirations of British Muslim girls', *British Journal of Guidance and Counselling*, 24, pp 227-42.

Basit, T.N. (1997) *Eastern Values, Western Milieu: Identities and Aspirations of Adolescent British Muslim girls*. Aldershot: Ashgate.

Battu, H. and Sloane, P.J. (2003) 'Educational mismatch and ethnic minorities in England and Wales', in F. Büchel, A de Grip and A. Mertens (eds) *Overeducation in Europe: Current Issues in Theory and Policy*. Cheltenham, UK and Northampton, MA: Edward Elgar, pp 217-35.

Battu, H. and Sloane, P.J. (2004) 'Over-education and ethnic minorities in Britain', *Manchester School*, 72(4), pp 535-59.

Battu, H., Mwale, M. and Zenou, Y. (2005) *Oppositional Identities and the Labour Market*. London: Centre for Economic Policy Research.

Battu, H., Seaman, P. and Zenou, Y. (2004) *Job Contact Networks and the Ethnic Minorities*, IUI Working Paper, vol 628. Stockholm: The Research Institute of Industrial Economics.

Bell, B.D. (1997) 'The performance of immigrants in the United Kingdom: evidence from the GHS', *Economic Journal*, 107(441), pp 333-344.

Berrington, A. (1994) 'Marriage and family formation among the white and ethnic minority populations in Britain', *Ethnic and Racial Studies*, 17, pp 517-45.

Berrington, A. (1996) 'Marriage patterns and inter-ethnic unions', in D. Coleman and J. Salt (eds) *Ethnicity in the 1991 Census: Volume One: Demographic Characteristics of the Ethnic Minority Populations*. London: HMSO, pp 178-212.

Berthoud, R. (1997) 'Income and standards of living', in T. Modood, R. Berthoud, J. Lakey, J. Nazroo, P. Smith, S. Virdee and S. Beishon (eds) *Ethnic Minorities in Britain: Diversity and Disadvantage*. London: PSI, pp 150-83.

Berthoud, R. (1998a) 'Defining ethnic groups: origin or identity?', *Patterns of Prejudice*, 32(2), pp 53-63.

Berthoud, R. (1998b) *The Incomes of Ethnic Minorities*, ISER Working Paper 98. Colchester: Institute for Social and Economic Research, University of Essex.

Berthoud, R. (1999) *Young Caribbean Men in the Labour Market: A Comparison with Other Ethnic Groups*. York: Joseph Rowntree Foundation.

Berthoud, R. (2000) 'Ethnic employment penalties in Britain', *Journal of Ethnic and Migration Studies*, 26(3): 389-416.

Berthoud, R. (2001) 'Teenage births to ethnic minority women', *Population Trends*, 104, pp 12-17.

Berthoud, R. (2005) 'Family formation in multicultural Britain: diversity and change', in G. C. Loury, T. Modood and S. M. Teles (eds) *Ethnicity, Social Mobility and Public Policy*. Cambridge: Cambridge University Press, pp 222-53.

Berthoud, R. (2006) *The Employment Rates of Disabled People*, DWP Research Report 298, Leeds: Leeds Corporate Document Services.

Berthoud, R. and Beishon, S. (1997) 'People, families and households', in T. Modood, R. Berthoud, J. Lakey, J. Nazroo, P. Smith, S. Virdee and S. Beishon (eds) *Ethnic Minorities in Britain: Diversity and Disadvantage*. London: PSI, pp 18-59.

Berthoud, R. and Blekesaune, M. (2006) *Persistent Employment Disadvantage, 1974 to 2003*, ISER Working Paper 2006-9. Colchester: University of Essex.

Bhattacharyya, G., Ison, L. and Blair, M. (2003) *Minority Ethnic Attainment and Participation in Education and Training: The Evidence*, Research Topic Paper, RTP01-03. London: DfES.

Bhavnani, R. (2006) *Ahead of the Game: The Changing Aspirations of Young Ethnic Minority Women*. Manchester: EOC.

Bhavnani, R., Mirza, H.S. and Meetoo, V. (2005) *Tackling the Roots of Racism: Lessons for Success*. Bristol: The Policy Press.

Bhopal, K. (1998) 'How gender and ethnicity intersect: the significance of education, employment and marital status', *Sociological Research Online*, 3(3), pp 1-16.

Blackaby, D.H., Drinkwater, S., Leslie, D.G. and Murphy, P.D. (1997) 'A picture of male and female unemployment among Britain's ethnic minorities', *Scottish Journal of Political Economy*, 44(2), pp 182-97.

Blackaby, D.H., Leslie, D.G., Murphy, P.D. and O'Leary, N.C. (1999) 'Unemployment among Britain's ethnic minorities', *Manchester School*, 67, pp 1-20.

Blackaby, D.H., Leslie, D.G., Murphy, P.D. and O'Leary, N.C. (2002) 'White/ethnic minority earnings and employment differentials in Britain: evidence from the LFS', *Oxford Economic Papers*, 54, pp 270-97.

Blackaby, D.H., Leslie, D.G., Murphy, P.D. and O'Leary, N.C. (2005) 'Born in Britain: how are native ethnic minorities faring in the British labour market', *Economics Letters*, 88, pp 370-5.

Blackwell, L. and Guinea-Martin, D. (2005) 'Occupational segregation by sex and ethnicity in England and Wales, 1991 to 2001', *Labour Market Trends*, 13(12), pp 501-11.

Bloch, A. (1993) *Access to Benefits: The Information Needs of Minority Ethnic Groups*. London: PSI.

Bloch, A. (1997) 'Ethnic inequality and social security', in A. Walker and C. Walker (eds) *Britain Divided: The Growth of Social Exclusion in the 1980s and 1990s*. London: CPAG, pp 111-22.

Boneham, M. (1997) 'Elderly people from ethnic minorities in Liverpool: mental illness, unmet need and barriers to service use', *Health and Social Care in the Community*, 5(3), pp 173-80.

Boneham, M. (2000) 'Shortchanging black and minority ethnic elders', in J. Bradshaw and R. Sainsbury (eds) *Experiencing Poverty*. Aldershot: Ashgate, pp 166-80.

Bonnett, A. (2000) *White Identities: Historical and International Perspectives*. Harlow: Pearson Education.

Bonnett, A. and Carrington, B. (2000) 'Fitting into categories or falling between them? Rethinking ethnic classification', *British Journal of Sociology of Education*, 21(4), pp 487-500.

Bosveld, K. and Connolly, H. (2006) 'Population', in J. Dobbs, H. Green and L. Zealey (eds) *Focus on Ethnicity and Religion*. Basingstoke: Palgrave, pp 19-42.

Botcherby, S. (2006) *Pakistani, Bangladeshi and Black Caribbean Women and Employment Survey: Aspirations, Experiences and Choices*. Manchester: EOC.

Bowes, A. and Sim, D. (1997) *Perspectives on Welfare: The Experiences of Minority Ethnic Groups in Scotland*. Aldershot: Ashgate.

Bowes, A. and Sim, D. (2002) 'Patterns of residential settlement among black and minority ethnic groups', in P. Somerville and A. Steele (eds) *'Race', Housing and Social Exclusion*. London: Jessica Kingsley, pp 40-60.

Bradford, B. (2006) *Who are the 'Mixed' Ethnic Groups?* London: Office for National Statistics.

Bradford, B. and Forsyth, F. (2006) 'Employment and labour market participation', in J. Dobbs, H. Green and L. Zealey (eds) *Focus on Ethnicity and Religion*. Basingstoke: Palgrave Macmillan, pp 111-58.

Bradley, S. and Taylor, J. (2004) 'Ethnicity, educational attainment and the transition from school', *Manchester School*, 72(3), pp 317-46.

Bradshaw, J., Finch, N., Mayhew, E., Ritakallio, V.-M. and Skinner, C. (2006) *Child Poverty in Large Families*. Bristol: The Policy Press for the Joseph Rowntree Foundation.

Brah, A. and Shaw, S. (1992) "Race' and 'culture' in the gendering of labour markets: South Asian young Muslim women and the labour market', *New Community*, 29, pp 441-58.

Brook, K. (2002) 'Trade union membership: an analysis of data from the autumn 2001 Labour Force Survey', *Labour Market Trends*, 110(7), pp 343-54.

Brown, C. (1984) *Black and White Britain: The Third PSI Survey*. London: Heinemann.

Brown, M.S. (2000) 'Religion and economic activity in the South Asian population', *Ethnic and Racial Studies*, 23(6), pp 1035-61.

Brown, U. (2000) *Race, Ethnicity and Poverty, Briefing Sheet 12, November 2000*. Glasgow: Scottish Poverty Information Unit.

Buck, N. (2001) 'Identifying neighbourhood effects on social exclusion', *Urban Studies*, 38(12), pp 2251-75.

Buck, N. (2004) *Newham Household Panel Survey: Household Income Poverty and Deprivation*. A report prepared by ISER, University of Essex, for the London Borough of Newham. London: London Borough of Newham.

Bulmer, M. (1996) 'The ethnic group question in the 1991 Census of population', in D. Coleman and J. Salt (eds) *Ethnicity in the 1991 Census: Volume One: Demographic characteristics of the Ethnic Minority Populations*. London: HMSO, pp 33-62.

Burton, D. (1997) 'Ethnicity and occupational welfare: a study of pension scheme membership', *Work, Employment and Society*, 11(3), pp 505-18.

Butt, J., Gorbach, P. and Ahmad, B. (1991) *Equally Fair? A Report on Social Services Departments' Development, Implementation and Monitoring of Services for the Black and Minority Ethnic Community.* London: Race Equality Unit.

Campbell, C. and McLean, C. (2003) 'Social capital, local community participation and the construction of Pakistani identities in England: implications for health inequalities policies', *Journal of Health Psychology*, 8(2), pp 247-62.

Card, D. (2005) 'Is the new immigration really so bad?', *The Economic Journal*, 115(507), pp F300-F323.

Carey, S. (2004) *Curry Capital: The Restaurant Sector in London's Brick Lane*, ICS Working Paper 6. London: Institute of Community Studies.

Carmichael, F. and Woods, R. (2000) 'Ethnic penalties in unemployment and occupational attainment: evidence for Britain', *International Review of Applied Economics*, 14(1), pp 71-98.

Carter, M. (1996) *Poverty and Prejudice: A Preliminary Report on the Withdrawal of Benefit Entitlement and the Impact of the Asylum and Immigration Bill.* London: Commission for Racial Equality/Refugee Council.

Cemlyn, S. and Clark, C. (2005) 'The social exclusion of Gypsy and Traveller children', in G. Preston (ed) *At Greatest Risk: The Children Most Likely to be Poor*, London: CPAG, pp 150-65.

Chance, J. (1996) 'The Irish: invisible settlers', in C. Peach (ed) *Ethnicity in the 1991 Census: Volume Two: The Ethnic Minority Populations of Great Britain*. London: HMSO, pp 221-39.

Chandola, T. (2001) 'Ethnic and class differences in health in relation to British South Asians: using the new National Statistics socio-economic classification', *Social Science and Medicine*, 51, pp 1285-96.

Chau, R.C.M. and Yu, S. (2001) 'Social exclusion of Chinese people in Britain', *Critical Social Policy*, 21(1), pp 103-25.

Cheng, Y. (1996) 'The Chinese: upwardly mobile', in C. Peach (ed) *Ethnicity in the 1991 Census: Volume Two: The Ethnic Minority Populations of Great Britain*, London: HMSO, pp 161-80.

Cheng, Y. and Heath, A. (1993) 'Ethnic origins and class destinations', *Oxford Review of Education*, 19(2), pp 151-66.

Clark, K. and Drinkwater, S. (1998) 'Ethnicity and self-employment in Britain', *Oxford Bulletin of Economic and Statistics*, 60, pp 383-407.

Clark, K. and Drinkwater, S. (2000) 'Pushed out or pulled in? Self-employment among ethnic minorities in England and Wales', *Labour Economics*, 7, pp 603-28.

Clark, K. and Drinkwater, S. (2002) 'Enclaves, neighbourhood effects and economic outcomes: ethnic minorities in England and Wales', *Journal of Population Economics*, 15, pp 5-29.

Clark, K. and Drinkwater, S. (2007) *Dynamics and Diversity: Ethnic Minorities in the Labour Market*, Bristol/York: The Policy Press/Joseph Rowntree Foundation.

Clark, K. and Lindley, J. (2004) 'Immigrant labour market assimilation and arrival effects: evidence from the Labour Force Survey', Paper presented at the Royal Economics Society Annual Conference, Swansea, 5-7 April, available at: http://ideas.repec.org/p/ecj/ac2004/68.html

Cohen, R., Coxall, J., Craig, G. and Sadiq-Sangster, A. (1992) *Hardship Britain: Being Poor in the 1990s.* London: CPAG.

Coleman, D. (1994) 'Trends in fertility and intermarriage among immigrant populations in Western Europe as measures of integration', *Journal of Biosocial Sciences*, 26, pp 107-36.

Coleman, D. and Salt, J. (eds) (1996a) *Ethnicity in the 1991 Census: Volume One: Demographic characteristics of the Ethnic Minority Populations.* London: HMSO.

Coleman, D. and Salt, J. (1996b) 'The ethnic group question in the 1991 Census: a new landmark in British social statistics', in D. Coleman and J. Salt (eds) *Ethnicity in the 1991 Census: Volume One: Demographic Characteristics of the Ethnic Minority Populations.* London: HMSO, pp 1-32.

Commission for Racial Equality (1996) *We Regret to Inform You.* London: Commission for Racial Equality.

Community Cohesion Review Team (2001) *Community Cohesion: A Report of the Independent Review Team Chaired by Ted Cantle.* London: Home Office.

Compton, P. (1996) 'Indigenous and older minorities', in D. Coleman and J. Salt (eds) *Ethnicity in the 1991 Census: Volume One: Demographic Characteristics of the Ethnic Minority Populations.* London: HMSO, pp 243-82.

Connolly, H. and Raha, C. (2006) 'Households and families', in J. Dobbs, H. Green and L. Zealey (eds) *Focus on Ethnicity and Religion.* Basingstoke: Palgrave Macmillan, pp 84-110.

Connolly, P. (2002) *'Race' and Racism in Northern Ireland: A Review of the Research Evidence*, Belfast: Office of the First Minister and Deputy First Minister.

Connolly, P. and Keenan, M. (2001) *The Hidden Truth: Racist Harassment in Northern Ireland*, Belfast: Northern Ireland Statistics and Research Agency.

Cornell, S. and Hartmann, D. (1998) *Ethnicity and Race: Making Identities in a Changing World.* Thousand Oaks, CA: Pine Forge Press.

CPAG (Child Poverty Action Group) (2002) *Migration and Social Security Handbook: A Rights Guide for People Entering and Leaving the UK* (3rd edition). London: CPAG.

Craig, G. (1999) "Race', social security and poverty', in J. Ditch (ed) *Introduction to Social Security: Policies, Benefits and Poverty.* London: Routledge, pp 206-26.

Craig, G. (2005) 'Poverty among black and minority ethnic children', in G. Preston (ed) *At Greatest Risk: The Children Most Likely to be Poor.* London: CPAG, pp 65-78.

Craig, P. and Greenslade, M. (1998) *First Findings from the Disability Follow Up to the Family Resources Survey: DSS Research Summary No 5.* London: DSS Social Research Branch.

Dale, A. (2002) 'Social exclusion of Pakistani and Bangladeshi women', *Sociological Research Online,* 7(3).

Dale, A., Dex, S. and Lindley, J.K. (2004) 'Ethnic differences in women's demographic, family characteristics and economic activity profiles, 1992 – 2002', *Labour Market Trends,* 112(4), pp 153-65.

Dale, A., Lindley, J. and Dex, S. (2006) 'A life-course perspective on ethnic differences in women's economic activity in Britain', *European Sociological Review,* 22(4), pp 459-76.

Dale, A., Williams, M. and Dodgeon, B. (1996) *Housing Deprivation and Social Change.* London: HMSO.

Dale, A., Shaheen, N., Fieldhouse, E. and Kalra, V. (2002) 'Labour market prospects for Pakistani and Bangladeshi women', *Work, Employment and Society,* 16(1), pp 5-25.

Daley, P. (1996) 'Black-Africans: students who stayed', in C. Peach (ed) *Ethnicity in the 1991 Census: Volume Two: The Ethnic Minority Populations of Great Britain.* London: HMSO, pp 44-65.

Daley, P.O. (1998) 'Black Africans in Great Britain: spatial concentration and segregation', *Urban Studies,* 35(10), pp 1703-24.

Daniel, W.W. (1968) *Racial Discrimination in England.* Harmondsworth: Penguin.

Davey Smith, G., Chaturvedi, N., Harding, S., Nazroo, J.Y. and Williams, J. (2000) 'Ethnic inequalities in health: a review of UK epidemiological evidence', *Critical Public Health,* 10(4), pp 375-408.

Denny, K.J., Harmon, C.P. and Roche, M.J. (1997) *The Distribution of Discrimination in Immigrant Earnings: Evidence from Britain 1974-93,* Institute for Fiscal Studies Working Paper 97/19. London: IFS.

DfES (Department for Education and Skills) (2005a) *Ethnicity and Education: The Evidence on Minority Ethnic Pupils,* Research Topic Paper, RTP01-05. London: DfES.

DfES (2005b) *Higher Standards, Better Schools For All: More Choice for Parents and Pupils.* London: The Stationery Office.

DH (Department of Health) (2003) *Tackling Health Inequalities: A Programme for Action.* London: DH.

DMAG (Data Management and Analysis Group) (2005) *Inter-ethnic Unions,* Census update, 2005/12. London: DMAG.

Dobbs, J., Green, H. and Zealey, L. (eds) (2006) *Focus on Ethnicity and Religion: 2006 Edition.* Basingstoke: Palgrave Macmillan.

Dorling, D. (1997) 'Regional and local differences in the housing tenure of ethnic minorities', in V. Karn (ed) *Ethnicity in the 1991 Census: Volume Four: Employment, Education and Housing among the Ethnic Minority Populations of Britain*. London: The Stationery Office, pp 147-69.

Dorling, D. (2005) *Human Geography of the UK*. London: Sage Publications.

Dorsett, R. (1998) *Ethnic Minorities in the Inner City*. Bristol/York: The Policy Press/Joseph Rowntree Foundation.

Drew, D. (1995) *'Race', Education and Work: The Statistics of Inequality*. Aldershot: Avebury.

Drew, D., Gray, J. and Sporton, D. (1997) 'Ethnic differences in the educational participation of 16-19 year olds', in V. Karn (ed) *Ethnicity in the 1991 Census: Volume Four: Employment, Education and Housing among the Ethnic Minority Populations of Britain*. London: The Stationery Office, pp 17-28.

Dudley, J., Roughton, M., Fidler, J. and Woollacott, S. (2005) *Control of Immigration: Statistics United Kingdom, 2004*. London: RDS, Home Office/National Statistics.

Duffield, M. (2002) 'Trends in female employment 2002', *Labour Market Trends*, 110(11), pp 605-16.

Dustmann, C. (1999) 'Temporary migration, human capital and language fluency of migrants', *Scandinavian Journal of Economics*, 101, pp 297-314.

Dustmann, C. and Fabbri, F. (2003) 'Language proficiency and labour market performance of immigrants in the UK', *Economic Journal*, 113(489), pp 695-717.

Dustmann, C. and Fabbri, F. (2005a) 'Immigrants in the British labour market', *Fiscal Studies*, 26(4), pp 423-70.

Dustmann, C. and Fabbri, F. (2005b) 'Gender and ethnicity: married immigrants in Britain', *Oxford Review of Economic Policy*, 21(3), pp 462-84.

Dustmann, C. and Theodoropoulos, N. (2006) *Ethnic Minority Immigrants and their Children in Britain*, CReAM Working Paper. London: UCL.

Dustmann, C. and van Soest, A. (2004) 'An analysis of speaking fluency of immigrants using ordered response models with classification errors', *Journal of Business and Economic Statistics*, 22(3), pp 312-21.

Dustmann, C., Fabbri, F. and Preston, I. (2005) 'The impact of immigration on the British labour market', *The Economic Journal*, 115(507), pp F324-F341.

DWP (Department for Work and Pensions) (2003) *Measuring Child Poverty*. London: DWP.

DWP (2005a) *Households Below Average Income 2003/04*. London: DWP.

DWP (2005b) *Opportunity for All: Seventh Annual Report 2005*. London: The Stationery Office.

DWP (2006a) *A New Deal for Welfare: Empowering People to Work*. London: The Stationery Office.

DWP (2006b) *Opportunity for All: Eighth Annual Report: 2006 Strategy Document*. London: The Stationery Office.

DWP (2006c) *Family Resources Survey, United Kingdom 2004-05*. London: DWP/National Statistics.

Eade, J., Vamplew, T. and Peach, C. (1996) 'The Bangladeshis: the encapsulated community', in C. Peach (ed) *Ethnicity in the 1991 Census: Volume Two: The Ethnic Minority Populations of Great Britain*. London: HMSO, pp 150-60.

Ermisch, J.F., Francesconi, M. and Pevalin, D.J. (2001) *Outcomes for Children of Poverty*. London: DWP.

Ethnic Minority Employment Task Force (2005) *Ethnic Minority Employment Task Force: Second Annual Report*, available at www.emetaskforce.gov.uk

Ethnos (2005) *Citizenship and Belonging: What is Britishness?* London: CRE.

Evandrou, M. (2000) 'Social inequalities in later life', *Population Trends*, 110, pp 11-18.

Fieldhouse, E. and Gould, M. (1998) 'Ethnic minority unemployment and local labour market conditions in Great Britain', *Environment and Planning*, 30, pp 833-53.

Fieldhouse, E. (1999) 'Ethnic minority unemployment and spatial mismatch: the case of London', *Urban Studies*, 36, pp 1569-96.

Fitzpatrick, P. (2005) 'Asylum seeker families', in G. Preston (ed) *At Greatest Risk: The Children Most Likely to be Poor*. London: CPAG, pp 92-108.

Flaherty, J., Veit-Wilson, J. and Dornan, P. (2004) *Poverty: The Facts* (5th edition). London: CPAG.

Frijters, P., Shields, M.A. and Wheatley Price, S. (2005) 'Job search methods and their success: a comparison of immigrants and natives in the UK', *The Economic Journal*, 115(507), pp F359-F376.

Frijters, P., Shields, M.A., Theodoropoulos, N. and Wheatley Price, S. (2004) *Testing for Employee Discrimination using Matched Employer–Employee Data: Theory and Evidence*, Department of Economics Research Paper 915. Melbourne: University of Melbourne.

Galster, G.C., Metzger, K. and Waite, R. (1999) 'Neighbourhood opportunity structures and immigrants' socioeconomic advancement', *Journal of Housing Research*, 10(1), pp 95-127.

Gardener, D. and Connolly, H. (2005) *Who are the 'Other' Ethnic Groups?* London: Office for National Statistics.

Gazioglu, S. (1996) 'English language proficiency and the earnings of Turkish and Bangladeshi immigrants in London', in S. Gazioglu (ed) *Migrants in the European Labour Market*. Aberdeen: J-Net, pp 62-84.

Geertz, C. (1993) *The Interpretation of Cultures*. London: Fontana Press.

Gillborn, D. and Mirza, H.S. (2000) *Educational Inequality: Mapping Race, Class and Gender: A Synthesis of Research Evidence*. London: OFSTED.

Gilroy, P. (2000) *Between Camps: Race, Identity and Nationalism at the End of the Colour Line*. Harmondsworth: Allen Lane/The Penguin Press.

Ginn, J. and Arber, S. (2000) 'Ethnic inequality in later life: variation in financial circumstances by gender and ethnic group', *Education and Ageing*, 15(1), pp 65-83.

Ginn, J. and Arber, S. (2001) 'Pension prospects of minority ethnic groups: inequalities by gender and ethnicity', *British Journal of Sociology*, 52(3), pp 519-39.

Gordon, D. and Pantazis, C. (1997) *Breadline Britain in the 1990s.* Aldershot: Ashgate.

Gordon, S., Sidell, R., Jones, P. and Lonsdale, J. (2002) *Tackling Pensioner Poverty: Encouraging Take-up of Entitlements.* London: National Audit Office.

Gordon, D., Levitas, R., Pantazis, C., Patsios, D., Payne, S., Townsend, P., Adelman, L., Ashworth, K., Middleton, S., Bradshaw, J. and Williams, J. (2000) *Poverty and Social Exclusion in Britain.* York: Joseph Rowntree Foundation.

Goulbourne, H. (1998) *Race Relations in Britain since 1945.* Basingstoke: Macmillan.

Green, A. (1997) 'Patterns of ethnic minority employment in the context of industrial and occupational growth and decline', in V. Karn (ed) *Ethnicity in the 1991 Census: Volume Four: Employment, Education and Housing among the Ethnic Minority Populations of Britain.* London: The Stationery Office, pp 67-90.

Gregg, P., Harkness, S. and Machin, S. (1999) *Child Development and Family Incomes.* York: York Publishing Services.

Gregg, P., Waldfogel, J. and Washbrook, E. (2005) *Expenditure Patterns Post-Welfare Reform in the UK: Are Low-income Families Starting to Catch Up?*, CASE Paper 99. London: Centre for Analysis of Social Exclusion, London School of Economics and Political Science.

Grenier, M. (1996) *The State of Asylum: A Critique of Asylum Policy in the UK.* London: The Refugee Council.

Harding, S. and Balarajan, R. (2000) 'Limiting long-term illness among Black Caribbeans, Black Africans, Indians, Pakistanis, Bangladeshis and Chinese born in the UK', *Ethnicity and Health*, 5(1), pp 41-6.

Harker, L. (2006) *Delivering on Child Poverty: What Would it Take?*, A report for the DWP, Cm 6951. London: The Stationery Office.

Harrison, M. (2003) 'Housing black and minority ethnic communities: diversity and constraint', in D. Mason (ed) *Explaining Ethnic Differences: Changing Patterns of Disadvantage in Britain.* Bristol: The Policy Press, pp 105-19.

Hatton, T.J. and Tani, M. (2005) 'Immigration and inter-regional mobility in the UK, 1982-2000', *The Economic Journal*, 115(507), pp F342-F358.

Hatton, T. J. and Wheatley Price, S. (2005) 'Migration, migrants and policy in the United Kingdom', in K. Zimmermann (ed) *European Migration: What do we Know?* Oxford: Oxford University Press, pp 113-72.

Heath, A. (2001) *Ethnic Minorities in the Labour Market.* London: Cabinet Office.

Heath, A. and Cheung, S.Y. (2006) *Ethnic Penalties in the Labour Market: Employers and Discrimination*, DWP Research Report 341. Leeds: Corporate Document Services.

Heath, A. and McMahon, D. (1997) 'Education and occupational attainments: the impact of ethnic origins', in V. Karn (ed) *Ethnicity in the 1991 Census: Volume Four: Employment, Education and Housing among The Ethnic Minority Populations of Britain*. London: HMSO, pp 91-113.

Heath, A. and McMahon, D. (2005) 'Social mobility of ethnic minorities', in G. C. Loury, T. Modood and S.M. Teles (eds) *Ethnicity, Social Mobility and Public Policy: Comparing the US and UK*. Cambridge: Cambridge University Press, pp 393-413.

Heath, A. and Smith, S. (2003) 'Mobility and ethnic minorities: levels of employment are greater cause for concern than social immobility', *New Economy*, 10(4), pp 199-204.

Heath, A. and Yu, S. (2005) 'Explaining ethnic minority disadvantage', in A. F. Heath, J. Ermisch and D. Gallie (eds) *Understanding Social Change*. Oxford: British Academy/Oxford University Press, pp 187-225.

Hickman, M.J. (2005) 'Ruling an empire, governing a multinational state: the impact of Britain's historical legacy on the ethno-racial regime', in G. C. Loury, T. Modood and S.M. Teles (eds) *Ethnicity, Social Mobility and Public Policy: Comparing the US and the UK*. Cambridge: Cambridge University Press, pp 21-49.

Hills, J., Le Grand, J. and Piachaud, D. (eds) (2002) *Understanding Social Exclusion*. Oxford: Oxford University Press.

HM Government (2006) *Reaching Out: An Action Plan on Social Exclusion*, London: Cabinet Office.

Holst, E. and Schrooten, M. (2006) *Migration and Money: What Determines Remittances? Evidence from Germany*, DIW Working Paper 566. Berlin: DIW.

Holzer, H.J. and Ihlanfeldt, K.R. (1998) 'Customer discrimination and employment outcomes for minority workers', *Quarterly Journal of Economics*, 113, pp 835-67.

Home Office (2004a) *Strength in Diversity: Towards a Community Cohesion and Race Equality Strategy*. London: Home Office.

Home Office (2004b) *The End of Parallel Lives? The Report of the Community Cohesion Panel*. London: Home Office.

Home Office (2005a) *Improving Opportunity, Strengthening Society: The Government's Strategy to Increase Race Equality and Community Cohesion*. London: Home Office.

Home Office (2005b) *Controlling our Borders: Making Migration Work for Britain: Five Year Strategy for Asylum and Immigration*. London: HMSO.

House of Commons Work and Pensions Committee (2005) *Department for Work and Pensions: Delivery of Services to Ethnic Minority Clients, Volume 1*. London: The Stationery Office.

Howard, K. (2006) 'Constructing the Irish of Britain: ethnic recognition and the 2001 UK censuses', *Ethnic and Racial Studies*, 29(1), pp 104-23.

Howes, E. and Mullins, D. (1997) 'Finding a place – the impact of locality on the housing experience of tenants from minority ethnic groups', in V. Karn (ed) *Ethnicity in the 1991 Census: Volume Four: Employment Education and Housing among the Ethnic Minority Populations of Britain*. London: The Stationery Office, pp 189-220.

Hudson, M., Barnes, H., Ray, K. and Phillips, J. (2006) *Ethnic Minority Perceptions and Experiences of Jobcentre Plus*, DWP Research Report 349. Leeds: Corporate Document Services.

Hussain, Y. and Bagguley, P. (2005) 'Citizenship, ethnicity and identity: British Pakistanis after the 2001 'riots'', *Sociology*, 39(3), pp 407-25.

Iacovou, M. and Berthoud, R. (2006) *The Economic Position of Large Families*, DWP Research Report 358. Leeds: Corporate Document Services.

Iganski, P. and Payne, G. (1996) 'Declining racial disadvantage in the British labour market', *Ethnic and Racial Studies*, 19(1), pp 113-34.

Iganski, P. and Payne, G. (1999) 'Socio-economic re-structuring and employment: the case of minority ethnic groups', *The British Journal of Sociology*, 50(2), pp 195-215.

IRIS Consulting (2005) *Department for Work & Pensions: Review of Race Equality and Public Sector Procurement*. London: DWP/Ethnic Minority Employment Task Force.

Jäckle, A. and Buck, N. (2005) *Newham Household Panel Survey: Household Income, Poverty and Deprivation*, A report prepared by ISER, University of Essex, for the London Borough of Newham. London: London Borough of Newham.

Jacobson, J. (1997) 'Religion and ethnicity: dual and alternative sources of identity among young British Pakistanis', *Ethnic and Racial Studies*, 20, pp 238-56.

Jacobson, J. (1998) *Islam in Transition: Religion and Identity among British Pakistani Youth*. London: Routledge.

Jenkins, S.P. and Rigg, J.A. (2001) *The Dynamics of Poverty in Britain*, DWP Research Report 157, London: DWP.

Jenkins, S.P., Micklewright, J. and Schnepf, S. V. (2006) 'Social segregation in secondary schools: how does England compare with other countries?', ISER Working Paper No. 2006-2. Colchester: University of Essex.

Johnson, S. and Fidler, Y. (2006) *Jobcentre Plus Customer Satisfaction: Ethnic Minority Booster Survey 2005*, DWP Research Report 338. Leeds: Corporate Document Services.

Karlsen, S. and Nazroo, J. (2002) 'Relation between racial discrimination, social class, and health among ethnic minority groups', *American Journal of Public Health*, 92(4), pp 624-31.

Karn, V. (ed) (1997) *Ethnicity in the 1991 Census: Volume Four: Employment, Education and Housing among the Ethnic Minority Populations of Britain*. London: The Stationery Office.

Karn, V., Dale, A. and Ratcliffe, P. (1997) 'Introduction: using the 1991 Census to study ethnicity', in V. Karn (ed) *Ethnicity in the 1991 Census: Volume Four: Employment, Education and Housing among the Ethnic Minority Populations of Britain.* London: The Stationery Office, pp xi–xxix.

Kempson, E. (1999) *Overcrowding in Bangladeshi Households: A Case Study of Tower Hamlets.* London: Policy Studies Institute.

Kim, N.K. (2005) 'The end of Britain? Challenges from devolution, European integration, and multiculturalism', *Journal of International and Area Studies*, 12(1), pp 61-80.

Kitchen, S., Michaelson, J., Wood, N. and John, P. (2006) *2005 Citizenship Survey: Race and Faith Topic Report.* London: Department for Communities & Local Government.

Kyambi, S. (2005) *Beyond Black and White: Mapping New Immigrant Communities.* London: Institute for Public Policy Research.

Lauglo, J. (2000) 'Social capital trumping class and cultural capital? Engagement with school among immigrant youth', in S. Baron, J. Field and T. Schuller (eds) *Social Capital: Critical Perspectives.* Oxford: Oxford University Press, pp 142-67.

Law, I. (1996) *Racism, Ethnicity and Social Policy.* London: Prentice Hall.

Law, I., Hylton, C., Karmani, A. and Deacon, A. (1994) *Racial Equality and Social Security Service Delivery: A Study of the Perceptions and Experiences of Black and Minority Ethnic People Eligible for Benefit in Leeds.* Leeds: University of Leeds.

Leslie, D. and Drinkwater, S. (1999) 'Staying on in full-time higher education: reasons for higher participation rates among ethnic minority males and females', *Economica*, 66(261), pp 63-77.

Leslie, D. and Lindley, J. (2001) 'The impact of language ability on employment and earnings of Britain's ethnic communities', *Economica*, 68(272), pp 587-606.

Lindley, J. (2002a) 'The English language fluency and earnings of ethnic minorities in Britain', *Scottish Journal of Political Economy*, 49(4), pp 467-87.

Lindley, J. (2002b) 'Race or religion? The impact of religion on the employment and earnings of Britain's ethnic communities', *Journal of Ethnic and Migration Studies*, 28(3), pp 427-42.

Lindley, J. (2005) 'Explaining ethnic unemployment and activity rates: evidence from the QLFS in the 1990s and 2000s', *Bulletin of Economic Research*, 57(2), pp 185-203.

Lindley, J., Dale, A. and Dex, S. (2006) 'Ethnic differences in women's employment: the changing role of qualifications', *Oxford Economic Papers*, 58, pp 351-78.

Lister, R. (2004) *Poverty.* Oxford: Blackwell.

Lloyd, E. (2006) 'Children, poverty and social exclusion', in C. Pantazis, D. Gordon and R. Levitas (eds) *Poverty and Social Exclusion in Britain: The Millennium Survey.* Bristol: The Policy Press, pp 315-46.

Longhi, S., Nijkamp, P. and Poot, J. (2006) *The Impact of Immigration on the Employment of Natives in Regional Labour Markets: A Meta-Analysis*, IZA Discussion Paper 2044. Bonn: IZA.

Lyon, N., Barnes, M. and Sweiry, D. (2006) *Families with Children in Britain: Findings from the 2004 Families and Children Study (FACS)*, DWP Research Report 340. Leeds: Corporate Document Services.

McIntosh, I., Sim, D. and Robertson, D. (2004) "We hate the English, except for you, cos you're our pal': identification of the 'English' in Scotland', *Sociology*, 38(1), pp 43-59.

Mack, J. and Lansley, S. (1985) *Poor Britain*. London: Allen & Unwin.

Mason, D. (2000) *Race and Ethnicity in Modern Britain* (2nd edition), Oxford: Oxford University Press.

Mason, D. (2003a) 'Changing ethnic disadvantage: an overview', in D. Mason (ed) *Explaining Ethnic Differences: Changing Patterns of Disadvantage in Britain*. Bristol: The Policy Press, pp 9-19.

Mason, D. (ed) (2003b) *Explaining Ethnic Differences: Changing Patterns of Disadvantage in Britain*. Bristol: The Policy Press.

Mason, D. (2003c) 'Changing patterns of ethnic disadvantage in employment', in D. Mason (ed) *Explaining Ethnic Differences: Changing Patterns of Disadvantage in Britain*. Bristol: The Policy Press, pp 69-86.

Mercorios, D. (1997) *Just Existence: A Report on the Lives of Asylum Seekers who have Lost Entitlement to Benefits in the UK*. London: Refugee Council.

Merkle, L. and Zimmermann, K.F. (1992) 'Savings, remittances and return migration', *Economics Letters*, 38, pp 77-81.

Middleton, S. and Ashworth, K. (1995) *Small Fortunes: National Survey of the Lifestyles and Living Standards of Children*. Loughborough: CRSP, University of Loughborough.

Modood, T. (1992) *Not Easy being British: Colour, Culture and Citizenship*. London: Runnymede.

Modood, T. (1997a) 'Culture and identity', in T. Modood, R. Berthoud, J. Lakey, J. Nazroo, P. Smith, S. Virdee and S. Beishon (eds) *Ethnic Minorities in Britain: Diversity and Disadvantage*. London: Policy Studies Institute, pp 290-338.

Modood, T. (1997b) 'Employment', in T. Modood, R. Berthoud, J. Lakey, J. Nazroo, P. Smith, S. Virdee and S. Beishon (eds) *Ethnic Minorities in Britain: Diversity and Disadvantage*. London: Policy Studies Institute, pp 83-149.

Modood, T. (1997c) 'Qualifications and English language', in T. Modood, R. Berthoud, J. Lakey, J. Nazroo, P. Smith, S. Virdee and S. Beishon (eds) *Ethnic Minorities in Britain: Diversity and Disadvantage*. London: Policy Studies Institute, pp 60-82.

Modood, T. (1998) 'Ethnic minorities' drive for qualifications', in T. Modood and T. Acland (eds) *Race and Higher Education: Experiences, Challenges and Policy Implications*. London: Policy Studies Institute, pp 24-38.

Modood, T., Beishon, S. and Virdee, S. (1994) *Changing Ethnic Identities*. London: Policy Studies Institute.

Modood, T., Berthoud, R. and Nazroo, J. (2002) 'Race, racism and ethnicity: a response to Ken Smith', *Sociology*, 36(2), pp 419-27.

Modood, T., Berthoud, R., Lakey, J., Nazroo, J., Smith, P., Virdee, S. and Beishon, S. (1997) *Ethnic Minorities in Britain: Diversity and Disadvantage*. London: Policy Studies Institute.

Moore, R. (2000) 'Material deprivation amongst ethnic minority and white children: the evidence of the Sample of Anonymised Records', in J. Bradshaw and R. Sainsbury (eds) *Experiencing Poverty*. Aldershot: Ashgate, pp 144-65.

Morris, L. and Ruane, S. (1989) *Household Finance Management and the Labour Market*. Aldershot: Ashgate.

National Association of Citizens Advice Bureaux (1996) 'Failing the test', *Benefits*, April/May, p 20.

National Statistics (2004a) *A Statistical Focus on Ethnicity in Wales*. Cardiff: Statistical Directorate, National Assembly for Wales.

National Statistics (2004b) *Focus on Ethnicity and Identity*. London: Office for National Statistics.

National Statistics (2006) *Social Trends 36*. London: National Statistics.

Nazroo, J. (1998) *The Health of Britain's Ethnic Minorities*. London: Policy Studies Institute.

Nazroo, J.Y. (2003) 'Patterns of and explanations for ethnic inequalities in health', in D. Mason (ed) *Explaining Ethnic Differences: Changing Patterns of Disadvantage in Britain*. Bristol: The Policy Press, pp 87-103.

Nesbitt, S. and Neary, D. (2001) *Ethnic Minorities and their Pension Decisions: A Qualitative Study of Pakistani, Bangladeshi and White Men in Oldham*. York: York Publishing Services.

Netto, G. (2006) 'Vulnerability to homelessness, use of services and homelessness prevention in black and minority ethnic communities', *Housing Studies*, 21(4), pp 585-605.

Netto, G., Fancy, C., Pawson, H., Lomax, D., Power, S. and Singh, S. (2004) *Black and Minority Ethnic Communities and Homelessness in Scotland*. Edinburgh: Scottish Executive.

Netto, G., Arshad, R., de Lima, P., Almeida Diniz, F., MacEwen, M., Patel, V. and Syed, R. (2001) *Audit of Research on Minority Ethnic Issues in Scotland from a 'Race' Perspective*. Edinburgh: Scottish Executive Central Research Unit.

Nolan, B. and Whelan, C. (1996) *Resources, Deprivation and Poverty*. Oxford: Clarendon Press.

Northern Ireland Statistics & Research Agency (2005) *Northern Ireland Multiple Deprivation Measure 2005*. London: The Stationery Office.

O'Leary, N.C., Murphy, P.D., Drinkwater, S.J. and Blackaby, D.H. (2001) 'English language fluence and the ethnic wage gap for men in England and Wales', *Economic Issues*, 6, pp 21-32.

ODPM (Office of the Deputy Prime Minister) (2004a) *Breaking the Cycle: Taking Stock of Progress and Priorities for the Future: A Report by the Social Exclusion Unit*. London: ODPM.

ODPM (2004b) *The English Indices of Deprivation 2004*. Wetherby: ODPM Publications.

Oldfield, N., Burr, S. and Parker, H.E. (2001) *Low Cost but Acceptable: A Minimum Income Standard for the UK: Muslim Families with Young Children*. London/York: Unison/Family Budget Unit.

ONS (Office for National Statistics) (2001) *Social Trends 31*. London: ONS.

ONS (2003) *Ethnic Group Statistics. A Guide for the Collection and Classification of Ethnicity Data*. London: HMSO.

ONS (2004) *Focus on Wales: Its People*. London: ONS.

ONS (2005) *Social Trends 35*. London: ONS.

Open Society Institute EU Monitoring and Advocacy Program (2004) *Aspirations and Reality: British Muslims and the Labour Market*. Budapest: Open Society Institute.

Owen, D. (1996a) 'Black-Other: the melting pot', in C. Peach (ed) *Ethnicity in the 1991 Census: Volume Two: The Ethnic Minority Populations of Great Britain*. London: HMSO, pp 66-94.

Owen, D. (1996b) 'The Other-Asians: the salad bowl', in C. Peach (ed) *Ethnicity in the 1991 Census: Volume Two: The Ethnic Minority Populations of Great Britain*. London: HMSO, pp 181-205.

Owen, D. (1997) 'Labour force participation rates, self-employment and unemployment', in V. Karn (ed) *Ethnicity in the 1991 Census: Volume Four: Employment, Education and Housing among the Ethnic Minority Populations of Britain*. London: The Stationery Office, pp 29-66.

Owen, D. and Green, A.E. (2000) 'Estimating commuting flows for minority ethnic groups in England and Wales', *Journal of Ethnic and Migration Studies*, 26(4), pp 581-608.

Owen, D. and Johnson, M. (1996) 'Ethnic minorities in the midlands', in P. Ratcliffe (ed) *Ethnicity in the 1991 Census: Volume Three: Social Geography and Ethnicity in Britain: Geographical Spread, Spatial Concentration and Internal Migration*. London: HMSO, pp 227-70.

Pantazis, C., Gordon, D. and Levitas, R. (eds) (2006) *Poverty and Social Exclusion in Britain: The Millennium Survey*. Bristol: The Policy Press.

Parekh, B. (2000) *The Future of Multi-Ethnic Britain* (The Parekh Report). London: Runnymede Trust/Profile Books.

Parker, H. (1998) *Low Cost but Acceptable: A Minimum Income Standard for the UK: Families with Young Children*. Bristol: The Policy Press.

Parker, H. (2001) *Low Cost but Acceptable: A Minimum Income Standard for Households with Children Living in London's East End*. London: Unison.

Payne, G. (2006) *Social Divisions* (2nd edition). Basingstoke: Palgrave Macmillan.

Peach, C. (ed) (1996a) *Ethnicity in the 1991 Census: Volume Two: The Ethnic Minority Populations of Great Britain*. London: HMSO.

Peach, C. (1996b) 'Black-Caribbeans: class, gender and geography', in C. Peach (ed) *Ethnicity in the 1991 Census: Volume Two: The Ethnic Minority Populations of Great Britain*. London: HMSO, pp 25-43.

Peach, C. (1996c) 'Does Britain have ghettos?', *Transactions of the Institute of British Geographers*, 21, pp 216-35.

Peach, C. (2005) 'Social integration and social mobility: segregation and intermarriage of the Caribbean population in Britain', in G. C. Loury, T. Modood and S. M. Teles (eds) *Ethnicity, Social Mobility and Public Policy: Comparing the US and UK*. Cambridge: Cambridge University Press, pp 178-203.

Peach, C. (2006) 'Muslims in the 2001 Census of England and Wales: gender and economic disadvantage', *Ethnic and Racial Studies*, 29(4), pp 629-55.

Peach, C. and Byron, M. (1994) 'Council house sales, residualisation and Afro-Caribbean tenants', *Journal of Social Policy*, 23(3), pp 363-83.

Peach, C. and Rossiter, D. (1996) 'Level and nature of spatial concentration and segregation of minority ethnic populations in Great Britain, 1991', in P. Ratcliffe (ed) *Ethnicity in the 1991 Census: Volume Three: Social Geography and Ethnicity in Britain: Geographical Spread, Spatial Concentration and Internal Migration*. London: HMSO, pp 111-34.

Pensions Commission (2004) *Pensions: Challenges and Choices: The First Report of the Pensions Commission*. London: The Stationery Office.

Phillips, D. (1997) 'The housing position of ethnic minority group home owners', in V. Karn (ed) *Ethnicity in the 1991 Census: Volume Four: Employment, Education and Housing among the Ethnic Minority Populations of Britain*. London: The Stationery Office, pp 170-88.

Phillips, D. (1998) 'Black minority ethnic concentration, segregation and dispersal in Britain', *Urban Studies*, 35(10), pp 1681-702.

Phillipson, C., Ahmed, N. and Latimer, J. (2003) *Women in Transition: A Study of the Experiences of Bangladeshi Women Living in Tower Hamlets*. Bristol: The Policy Press.

Platt, L. (2002) *Parallel Lives? Poverty among Ethnic Minority Groups in Britain*. London: Child Poverty Action Group.

Platt, L. (2003a) *Newham Household Panel Survey: Poverty and Deprivation in Newham*, A report prepared by ISER, University of Essex, for the London Borough of Newham. London: London Borough of Newham.

Platt, L. (2003b) 'Ethnicity and inequality: British children's experience of means-tested benefits', *Journal of Comparative Family Studies*, 34(3), pp 357-77.

Platt, L. (2003c) 'Social security in a multi-ethnic society', in J. Millar (ed) *Understanding Social Security: Issues for Social Policy and Practice*. Bristol: The Policy Press, pp 255-76.

Platt, L. (2005a) *Migration and Social Mobility: The Life Chances of Britain's Minority Ethnic Communities*. Bristol: The Policy Press.

Platt, L. (2005b) 'The intergenerational social mobility of minority ethnic groups', *Sociology*, 39(3), pp 445-61.

Platt, L. (2005c) 'New destinations? Assessing the post-migration social mobility of minority ethnic groups in England and Wales', *Social Policy and Administration*, 39(6), pp 697-721.

Platt, L. (2006a) *Assessing the Impact of Illness, Caring and Ethnicity on Social Activity*, CASE paper 108, London: Centre for Analysis of Social Exclusion, STICERD, London School of Economics and Political Science.

Platt, L. (2006b) 'Poverty', in G. Payne (ed) *Social Divisions* (2nd edition). London: Palgrave Macmillan, pp 275-304.

Platt, L. (2006c) 'Poverty and inequality', in J. Scott (ed) *Key Sociological Concepts.* London: Routledge, pp 123-7.

Platt, L. (2006d) *Pay Gaps: The Position of Ethnic Minority Men and Women.* Manchester: EOC.

Platt, L. (2006e) 'Social insecurity: children and benefit dynamics', *Journal of Social Policy,* 35(3), pp 391-410.

Platt, L. (2006f) *Ethnicity and Child Poverty*, Report prepared for the Ethnic Minority Employment Task Force, available at: www.emetaskforce.gov.uk/publications.asp

Platt, L. and Noble, M. (1999) *Race, Place and Poverty: Ethnic Groups and Low Income Distributions.* York: YPS for the Joseph Rowntree Foundation.

Platt, L. and Thompson, P. (2006) 'The role of family background and social capital in the social mobility of migrant ethnic minorities', in R. Edwards, J. Franklin and J. Holland (eds) *Assessing Social Capital: Concept, Policy and Practice.* Cambridge: Scholars Press, pp 191-217.

Platt, L., Simpson, L. and Akinwale, B. (2005) 'Stability and change in ethnic group in England and Wales', *Population Trends*, 121, pp 35-46.

Portes, A., Fernández-Kelly, P. and Haller, W. (2005) 'Segmented assimilation on the ground: the new second generation in early adulthood', *Ethnic and Racial Studies*, 28(6), pp 1000-40.

Pudney, S. and Shields, M.A. (2000) 'Gender, race, pay and promotion in the British nursing profession: estimation of a generalised ordered probit model', *Journal of Applied Econometrics*, 15(4), pp 367-99.

Ratcliffe, P. (1994) *'Race', Ethnicity and Nation.* London: UCL Press.

Ratcliffe, P. (ed) (1996a) *Ethnicity in the 1991 Census: Volume Three: Social Geography and Ethnicity in Britain: Geographical Spread, Spatial Concentration and Internal Migration.* London: HMSO.

Ratcliffe, P. (1996b) 'Introduction: social geography and ethnicity: a theoretical, conceptual and substantive overview', in P. Ratcliffe (ed) *Ethnicity in the 1991 Census: Volume Three: Social Geography and Ethnicity in Britain: Geographical Spread, Spatial Concentration and Internal Migration.* London: HMSO, pp 1-22.

Ratcliffe, P. (1997) "Race', ethnicity and housing differentials in Britain', in V. Karn (ed) *Ethnicity in the 1991 Census: Volume Four: Employment, Education and Housing among the Ethnic Minority Populations of Britain.* London: The Stationery Office, pp 130-46.

Rees, P. and Phillips, D. (1996) 'Geographical patterns in a cluster of Pennine cities', in P. Ratcliffe (ed) *Ethnicity in the 1991 Census: Volume Three: Social Geography and Ethnicity in Britain: Geographical Spread, Spatial Concentration And Internal Migration.* London: HMSO, pp 271-93.

Rendall, M. and Ball, D. (2004) 'Immigration, emigration and the ageing of the overseas-born population in the United Kingdom', *Population Trends*, 116, pp 18-27.

Rex, J. and Moore, R. (1967) *Race, Community and Conflict: A Study of Sparkbrook.* Oxford: Oxford University Press.

Reynolds, T. (2001) 'Black mothering, paid work and identity', *Ethnic and Racial Studies*, 24(6), pp 1046-64.

Roberts, C. and Campbell, S. (2006) *Talk on Trial: Job Interviews, Language and Ethnicity*, DWP Research Report 344. Leeds: Corporate Document Services.

Robinson, D. (2005) 'The search for community cohesion: key themes and dominant concepts of the public policy agenda', *Urban Studies*, 42(8), pp 1411-27.

Robinson, V. (1996a) 'The Indians: onward and upward', in C. Peach (ed) *Ethnicity in the 1991 Census: Volume Two: The Ethnic Minority Populations of Great Britain.* London: HMSO, pp 95-120.

Robinson, V. (1996b) 'Inter-generational differences in ethnic settlement patterns', in C. Peach (ed) *Ethnicity in the 1991 Census: Volume Three: Social Geography and Ethnicity in Britain: Geographical Spread, Spatial Concentration and Internal Migration.* London: HMSO, pp 175-99.

Robson, K. and Berthoud, R. (2003) *Early Motherhood and Disadvantage: A Comparison between Ethnic Groups*, ISER Working Paper 2003-29, Colchester: ISER, University of Essex.

Rothon, C. and Heath, A. (2003) 'Trends in racial prejudice', in A. Park, J. Curtice, K. Thomson, L. Jarvis and C.A. Bromley (eds) *British Social Attitudes: The 20th Report.* London: Sage Publications, pp 189-214.

Sadiq-Sangster, A. (1992) *Living on Income Support: An Asian Experience.* London: Family Services Unit.

Salt, J. (1996) 'Immigration and ethnic group', in D. Coleman and J. Salt (eds) *Ethnicity in the 1991 Census: Volume One: Demographic Characteristics of the Ethnic Minority Populations.* London: HMSO, pp 124-50.

Salway, S., Platt, L., Chowbey, P., Harriss, K. and Bayliss, E. (2007) *Long-term Ill Health, Poverty and Ethnicity*, Bristol/York: The Policy Press/Joseph Rowntree Foundation.

Sammons, P. (1995) 'Gender, ethnic and socio-economic differences in attainment and progress: a longitudinal analysis of student achievement over nine years', *British Educational Research Journal*, 21(4), pp 465-85.

Scottish Executive (2001) *Ethnic Minority Research Bulletin No. 1.* Edinburgh: Scottish Executive.

Scottish Executive (2004) *Analysis of Ethnicity in the 2001 Census: Summary Report.* Edinburgh: Office of the Chief Statistician, Scottish Executive, available at: www. scotland.gov.uk/library5/social/aescr-00.asp

Shields, M.A. and Wheatley Price, S. (1998) 'The earnings of male immigrants in England: evidence from the quarterly LFS', *Applied Economics*, 30, pp 1157-68.

Shields, M.A. and Wheatley Price, S. (1999) 'Ethnic differences in British employer-funded on and off-the-job training', *Applied Economics Letters*, 6, pp 421-9.

Shields, M.A. and Wheatley Price, S. (2001) 'Language fluency and immigrant employment prospects: evidence from Britain's ethnic minorities', *Applied Economics Letters*, 8, pp 741-5.

Shields, M.A. and Wheatley Price, S. (2002) 'The English language fluency and occupational success of ethnic minority immigrant men living in English metropolitan areas', *Journal of Population Economics*, 15, pp 137-60.

Simpson, L. (2005) 'On the measurement and meaning of residential segregation: a reply to Johnston, Poulsen and Forrest', *Urban Studies*, 42(7), pp 1229-30.

Simpson, N. (1991) 'Equal treatment? Black claimants and social security', *Benefits*, September/October, p 14.

Sly, F., Thair, T. and Risdon, A. (1998) 'Labour market participation of ethnic groups', *Labour Market Trends*, December, pp 601-15.

Smith, A. (2002) 'The new ethnicity classification in the Labour Force Survey', *Labour Market Trends*, 110(12), pp 657-66.

Smith, A.D. (1991) *National Identity.* Harmondsworth: Penguin.

Smith, D.J. (1977) *Racial Disadvantage in Britain: The PEP Report.* Harmondsworth: Penguin.

Somerville, P. and Steele, A. (2002) *'Race', Housing and Social Exclusion.* London: Jessica Kingsley.

Spence, L. (2005) *Country of Birth and Labour Market Outcomes in London: An Analysis of Labour Force Survey and Census Data*, DMAG Briefing 2005/1. London: Greater London Authority.

Storkey, M. and Lewis, R. (1996) 'London: a true cosmopolis', in P. Ratcliffe (ed) *Ethnicity in the 1991 Census: Volume Three: Social Geography and Ethnicity in Britain: Geographical Spread, Spatial Concentration and Internal Migration.* London: HMSO, pp 201-25.

Strategy Unit (2003) *Ethnic Minorities and the Labour Market.* London: Strategy Unit.

Tackey, N.D., Casebourne, J., Aston, J., Ritchie, H., Sinclair, A., Tyers, C., Hurstfield, J., Willison, R. and Page, R. (2006) *Barriers to Employment for Pakistanis and Bangladeshis in Britain*, DWP Research Report 360. Leeds: Corporate Document Services.

The Equalities Review (2006) *Interim Report for Consultation.* London: The Equalities Review.

Thomas, J.M. (1998) 'Who feels it knows it: work attitudes and excess non-white unemployment in the UK', *Ethnic and Racial Studies*, 21, pp 138-50.

Townsend, P. (1979) *Poverty in the United Kingdom: A Survey of Household Resources and Standards of Living.* Harmondsworth: Penguin.

Townsend, P. and Davidson, N. (1982) *Inequalities in Health: The Black Report,* Harmondsworth: Penguin.

TUC (Trades Union Congress) (2000) *Exposing Racism at Work.* London: TUC.

Turley, C. and Thomas, A. (2006) *Housing Benefit and Council Tax Benefit as In-work Benefits: Claimants' and Advisors' Knowledge, Attitudes and Experiences,* DWP Research Report 383. Leeds: Corporate Document Services.

Tyrer, D. and Ahmad, F. (2006) *Muslim Women and Higher Education: Identities, Experiences and Prospects.* Liverpool: Liverpool John Moores University and the ESF.

Walling, A. (2004) 'Workless households: results from the spring 2004 LFS', *Labour Market Trends,* 112(11), pp 435-45.

Walls, P. (2001) 'Religion, ethnicity and nation in the census: some thoughts on the inclusion of Irish ethnicity and Catholic religion', *Radical Statistics,* 78, pp 48-62.

Wayne, N. (2003) *Out of Sight: Race Inequality in the Benefits System.* London: Disability Alliance.

Weber, M. (1978) *Economy and Society* (edited by G. Roth and C. Wittich). Berkeley, CA: University of California Press.

Wheatley Price, S. (2001a) 'The employment adjustment of male immigrants in England', *Journal of Population Economics,* 14(1), pp 193-220.

Wheatley Price, S. (2001b) 'The unemployment experience of male immigrants in England', *Applied Economics,* 33, pp 201-15.

Wilkinson, R. (1996) *Unhealthy Societies: The Afflictions of Inequality,* London: Routledge.

Wilkinson, R. (2005) *The Impact of Inequality: How to Make Sick Societies Healthier,* New York, NY: The New Press.

Williams, R. and Harding, S. (2004) 'Poverty, stress and racism as factors in South Asian heart disease', in K. Patel and R. Bhopal (eds) *The Epidemic of Coronary Heart Disease in the South Asian Population: Causes and Consequences,* London: South Asian Health Foundation, pp 135-43.

Wilson, D., Burgess, S. and Briggs, A. (2005) *The Dynamics of School Attainment of England's Ethnic Minorities,* Centre for Market and Public Organisation (CMPO) Working Paper No 05/130. Bristol: University of Bristol.

Zetter, R., Griffiths, D., Sigona, N., Flynn, D., Pasha, T. and Beynon, R. (2006) *Immigration, Social Cohesion and Social Capital: What are the Links?* York: Joseph Rowntree Foundation.

Zhou, M. and Xiong, Y.S. (2005) 'The multifaceted American experiences of Asian immigrants: lessons for segmented assimilation', *Ethnic and Racial Studies,* 28(6), pp 1119-52.

Index

Page references for figures and tables are in *italics*; those for notes are followed by n